Living THE AIRSTREAM LIFE

KAREN FLETT

HARPER DESIGN

An Imprint of HarperCollinsPublishers

A JOURNEY TO FIND ADVENTURE

I grew up constructing forts in my backyard, creating hideouts in my attic escape hatch in my bedroom, or making a home in a secret hallway that my dad built from one end of the house to the other. Before long my dreams of adventures grew past their boundaries and I became a nomad among the trees and through the tunnels painstakingly cut through the thick bracken that covered acres of our backyard. As you can tell, I was a bit of an adventurer at a young age. I spent most of my time creating, discovering, and imagining, and usually I returned for dinner covered in scratches, dirt, and with nature's treasures dreadlocked into my curly hair.

Not much has changed in my years. I still love adventure, new experiences, and spending hours imagining, dreaming, and creating. The world just got bigger; the confines of the acres of our family farmland has now become the far-reaching ends of the earth. It's taken me a long time to truly understand that adventuring is what makes my soul light up and my heart open. Something I already knew as a child, but somehow those messages got lost and buried along the way.

I am very lucky to have parents who are adventurers. One parent's adventures are planned months in advance to make the most of every opportunity, traveling for months on end each year to discover the world's treasures. And the other parent's spontaneity and yearning for emotive experience and sincere value has given her a wealth of experience and knowledge far beyond what I can truly know. I couldn't have asked for more honest and sincere guides in life—polar opposites, I am finding my place in the middle—I couldn't be more grateful for the adventurous spirit they have instilled in me.

I yearn for adventure, to travel, to see and meet people of all different cultures and backgrounds. To appreciate the places that Mother Nature has created, and center myself among the varied landscapes that this world has to offer. But I also love home, I love the familiar feel, the comfort in the small things, and the safe haven of the expected. I have spent many years going back and forth between the "home" and the "unknown," all the while trying to balance one with the other. But my newest discovery allows me to find both, at the same time, in the same place.

Traveling with my home is where I find both comfort and experience. With the ability to hitch up my home and take it with me on my adventure, I find the nervous excitement of the unknown, yet travel with the comforting experience of the familiar. Airstream's founder, Wally Byam, knew this long before I had my own lightbulb moment; he didn't just take his trailers to the RV park—he went to Africa and South America, and traveled from one side of the world to the other, all the while taking the comforts of home.

Of course I love Airstreams for their unique shape and their exquisite design, but they connect with my soul because they embody the wanderer's connection to all that surrounds them; they attract kindred spirits who aren't content with sitting at home in an armchair, who want to live the gift of life they have been given, and feel both blessed and honored to have the opportunity to make the most of it. We live in an era when we are so lucky to be able to see beyond our needs, to see our desires. To be appreciative of that and to make the most of this wondrous opportunity will make us feel that we have truly lived our lives rather than just letting the days pass us by.

NOT ALL THOSE WHO WANDER ARE LOST.

J. R. R. TOLKIEN

CONTENTS

THE OPEN ROAD

WHY WOULD YOU LIVE OR VACATION IN A TRAILER?

Airstream's founder, Wally Byam, believed that traveling via trailer makes us "goodwill ambassadors." Those who dare to reach out beyond their comfort zone to be in different environments, meet new people, and share each other's stories and experiences, all the while taking the comforts of home with them in a beautifully designed Airstream trailer.

Traveling in a trailer allows you to make connections to the environment, the community, and the culture and history of the places you travel. We live a fast-paced lifestyle that influences the way in which we travel. We try to fit everything in at once and tick off the top ten sights we have been told to, and then move on to the next place on our fast-paced itinerary.

Traveling in a trailer allows you to stop, take the time to understand your surroundings, respond to the environment, create your plans as you go, and make the most of opportunities that come your way. It's like an open door to adventure and new experiences.

Rowan and Mark Sommerset are writers of beautiful children's books. They live full time in their Airstream trailer with their son, Linden. Quite new to this adventure, they are loving the learning curve and enjoying all the world has to offer through their Airstream lifestyle. Check out their website, *www.dreamboatbooks.com*, to learn more about their books and their journey. Above is the view of Mount Ngauruhoe in New Zealand from the Sommersets' Airstream, and to the right is their Airstream parked for the night in Evans Bay, Wellington, New Zealand.

WHY LIVING SMALL GIVES YOU THE CHOICES TO LIVE BIG

Choosing to live small in a trailer (or another type of small space) has many benefits. The positives are obvious: less overhead, less clutter, fewer financial commitments, less stress, and more time. But one of the often overlooked benefits is learning more about yourself through having the time and perspective to consider the bigger picture, rather than having to focus on the chores of daily living.

You learn to enjoy the here and now, to break the routine and expect the unexpected. Remember when you were a little kid how long an hour used to seem? You were learning new things all the time, no moment was the same, and you were always challenged. But as you get older, even if you're lucky enough to "learn a new thing every day," you settle into a repetitive routine all too easily. Start challenging yourself to live your life and break your routine. Get on the road and discover the never-ending learning experiences around every bend, and choose to live every day like it's a gift and not just part of a constant routine.

Making positive contributions to the world can begin by being a "conscious consumer." Since you'll need to make the most of your space, you will need to choose wisely what you put in it. Additionally, those who live this lifestyle for a long period of time find other ways to make positive contributions: figuring out what their true skills are and how to use them to be a productive member of society rather than having to focus on paying a massive mortgage and credit payments, or keeping

up with all the chores of modern-day living. By being able to be in the "here and now," enjoy the moment, and be grateful for the little things, they learn to see how to truly make a difference.

Airstream artist and renovator Elizabeth Jose and her partner, Raymon Belian. You can find some of her beautiful Airstream artwork featured on the covers of Airstream Life magazine, and check out her latest work on her Instagram site @elizjoseartist.

 **TOP 6** # REASONS TO LIVE AND TRAVEL IN A SMALL SPACE

1

Less Maintenance

The cost and time required to maintain a traditional house can consume your entire weekend, as well as your savings. A tiny space needs much less attention to maintenance and cleaning.

2

Better Health

Less need for money means less stress and more free time, and therefore more time spent on better health choices and happiness.

3

Flexibility

Less commitment to work requirements means you will have the ability to choose your path when opportunities arrive. You can be spontaneous and follow your nose to new adventures.

4

Less Debt

Less of your finances invested in your home and more efficient use of the income that you do have can lead to a life of being debt-free. You can manage to buy a tiny home outright in a tenth of the time it takes to pay off the mortgage on a traditional house.

5

More Time

You can enjoy being with loved ones, participating in a community, and following your passions. This will all add to the quality of your life.

6

Life Simplification

You will need to declutter your life to live tiny— you will simplify your chores and your needs and become a more thoughtful and conscious consumer of stuff.

Home sweet home to Matt Hackney, WBCCI Region 3 president, and his wife, Beth.

THE AIRSTREAM WAY OF LIFE

WHY AN AIRSTREAM?

The uniqueness of the exterior shape, the shiny silver, and the timeless design are often the first things that people notice about an Airstream. But the thing that makes them fall in love with an Airstream is the spirit in which they were created and the intention for their use. Wally Byam, the founder of Airstream, was an adventurer with a desire for learning about the unknown and experiencing unseen places.

WALLY BYAM

"STRIVE ENDLESSLY TO STIR THE VENTURESOME SPIRIT THAT MOVES YOU TO FOLLOW A RAINBOW TO ITS END . . . AND THUS MAKE YOUR TRAVEL DREAMS COME TRUE."

Airstream today is still built on this philosophy, and it resonates through the Airstream community to its very heart.

The Airstream Way of Life

Wally Byam never had a marketing division. He had what he called the "Airstream Way of Life" department. He was not set on selling you a trailer but on sharing with you the way of life he lived and enjoyed.

WALLY BYAM

"WE DON'T SELL TRAILERS; WE SELL A WAY OF LIFE."

The "Airstream way of life" is one filled with open doors and opportunities, new possibilities, new learning experiences, new people, new places, and new connections. It's the ability to step outside your comfort zone, while taking a little bit of home with you.

WALLY BYAM

Wally Byam was the epitome of the self-made man. He had a belief in himself and his abilities, and took every opportunity life gave him, with both hands. He was of strong character and was a great leader. Born in 1896 in Baker City, Oregon, he spent his youth traveling with his grandfather in a mule-drawn wagon. As he grew older he worked as a shepherd, living many a day in a shepherd's cart, far from civilization. Wally's growing love for the outdoors became a keystone for his life's successes. From early on he had a sense of adventure and independence, and he knew in his heart that he would be the leader of his own destiny.

Wally Byam addressing a WBCCI Rally, accompanied by Chica, his and Stella's Irish setter. Palm Springs, 1957.

Wally Byam and his wife, Stella, in their Airstream on the 1956 European caravan.

Airstream Beginnings

Airstream was officially founded by Wally Byam in 1931. His aspirations and love of travel and adventures, along with his wife's refusal to sleep on the ground in a tent, created the need for Airstream's first travel trailer.

Wally had built his first trailer in the late '20s, testing ways he could make the perfect homemade travel trailer for his personal use. He settled on a teardrop-shaped trailer with a rigid structure atop a Model T chassis, and he and his wife took to the road. Wally saw the growing interest in trailers, so he placed an ad in *Popular Mechanics* magazine, selling his trailer plans for a tidy sum of five dollars.

Many adventurers bought the plans to build their own trailers, although other people asked for trailer-kit sets to accompany the plans, or even the option of buying a completed trailer shell. Wally obliged, and began releasing the sets and building trailer shells in his backyard. He struggled to keep up with demand for his trailers, so much that he even survived the financial crash of 1929.

Wally opened up his first Airstream factory in 1931. He had a dream to create a lightweight travel trailer that was easy to tow, made with high-quality materials, and built with exceptional craftsmanship.

WALLY BYAM

"AIRSTREAMS ARE HANDCRAFTED, NOT HANDMADE."

In 1936, Airstream released the Clipper. With its aluminum-and-rivets frame and rounded shape, the foundation for the iconic Airstream trailer design had made its debut.

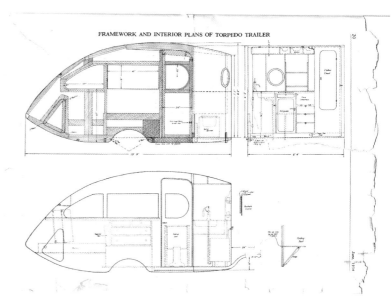

FRAMEWORK AND INTERIOR PLANS OF TORPEDO TRAILER

Wally's trailer plans that he sold for five dollars so any budding trailer-maker could follow in his footsteps.

The Airstream Factory at 1755 North Main Street, Los Angeles, home of the Airstream after WWII.

International Caravans

As Airstream began to really make its own mark in the late '40s and early '50s, attracting people from far and wide, Wally noticed one thing that struck him as peculiar: many people were buying Airstreams but not taking them far from home. When Wally discovered Airstreams were often left sitting in front yards, as their owners were a bit nervous about getting out on the open road, he began instigating the caravan: a group of trailers that go on a journey together, traveling one behind another to their destination.

Airstream caravans have become an integral part of the Airstream way of life since they started in the 1950s. Some of the famous caravans Wally led include the 1951 caravan to Mexico and Central America, the 1959 caravan from Cape Town to Cairo, and the around-the-world caravan in 1963, covering more than 31,000 miles over 403 days, starting in Singapore and ending in Lisbon, Portugal.

Caravans are a wonderful way of seeing the world outside your doorstep with a group of kindred spirits. Even though we no longer have Wally to lead us, caravans are still organized today, either officially through the WBCCI or as a group of like-minded individuals sharing a journey.

Above: 1956 European caravan. Below: 1949 Airstream Liners and their owners.

Helen and Wally celebrate both Wally's birthday and the Fourth of July amid the WBCCI 1960 international rally in Colorado Springs, Colorado.

WBCCI and Helen Byam Schwamborn

The Wally Byam Caravan Club was founded during a caravan through eastern Canada in 1955. On August 3, the caravan was in Kentville, Nova Scotia, and the travelers decided to make an official club to bring together the owners of Airstreams. Helen Byam Schwamborn (Wally's cousin) was one of the founding members of the WBCCI, and she established the headquarters and the club newsletter, the *Blue Beret*. Helen became integral to the planning and implementation of the caravans, including the African caravan in which her son, Dale, took part when he was only twenty. Helen became Wally's right-hand woman; he trusted her with many aspects of the business, including building and supporting the Airstream community. This community and the WBCCI backed Airstream through tough times, and without them, some believe, Airstream might have met its end in the coming years.

WBCCI also organized rallies, gatherings of Airstreamers from all corners of the United States. WBCCI still exists today, based out of an office just down the road from the Airstream factory in Jackson Center, Ohio. Members continue to hold caravans and regional rallies, and are brought together every year by the international rally.

This wonderful circular formation at a WBCCI international rally offered a communal meeting space in the middle and a sight to behold from the skies.

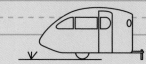

HISTORY OF THE AIRSTREAM

1929

FIRST TRAILER CREATED

Wally creates his first trailer.

1931

AIRSTREAM FACTORY OPENS

Airstream opens a small trailer factory in Culver City, California.

AIRSTREAM TORPEDO CAR CRUISER RELEASED

The Airstream Torpedo Car Cruiser is released, the first trailer to be mass produced from the new factory. It is also released as a kit set, a trailer shell, or as a set of plans in which the DIY enthusiast could build their own and add their own touch.

1936

AIRSTREAM CLIPPER RELEASED

The Clipper represents Airstream's first step toward the semi-monocoque aluminum framework that has become a renowned Airstream design.

1944

WORLD WAR II

During the war, aluminum is at a premium for making aircrafts and therefore becomes very hard to come by for travel trailers. In fact, the government ends up making it illegal for recreational trailer use.

Wally closes down Airstream during the years of the war, but like many in the trailer profession he takes up work in aircraft manufacturing. There he develops skills he will later put to use in the creation of Airstream trailers.

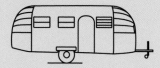

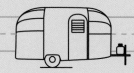

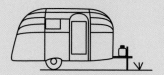

1946

CURTIS WRIGHT CLIPPER

During the war, Wally worked for airplane manufacturer Curtis Wright, and after the war ends, they work together to create the Curtis Wright Clipper.

1947

AIRSTREAM REOPENS

Wally decides to reopen Airstream at the North Main Street factory in Los Angeles, producing the Airstream Liner.

LETOURNEUR VISITS

Wally invites the famous French bicyclist Letourneur to visit the factory and pull an Airstream Liner with his bike, to showcase how light the trailers are. This picture will become the basis for the famous Airstream logo.

1951

THE FIRST CARAVAN

Wally creates and participates in a publicity marvel: the first international caravan, a group of trailers traveling together. They head south to Mexico and Central America.

1952

JACKSON CENTER FACTORY OPENS

Airstream opens its factory in Jackson Center, Ohio, where all Airstream trailers are still being made today.

1955

WBCCI FOUNDED

Wally Byam Caravan Club (International) is founded during a caravan in Canada.

1957

PANEL NUMBERS REDUCED

Technological advances in metalworking allow Airstream to reduce the number of panels used in the end caps from thirteen to seven.

SELF-CONTAINED TRAVEL TRAILER

Airstream introduces the International, the first ever "self-contained" travel trailer, which doesn't require external hookups.

1959

WBCCI CARAVAN

One of the most famous WBCCI caravans travels through Africa, from Cape Town to Cairo.

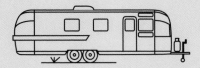

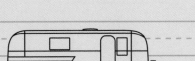

1961

BAMBI
TRAILER

Airstream introduces the Bambi, the smallest "self-contained" trailer available, at sixteen feet.

1962

WALLY
PASSES AWAY

On July 22, Wally Byam passes away. Art Costello becomes the new president of Airstream.

1969

EXTERIOR
REDESIGN

The Airstream trailer undergoes a major redesign, creating a much rounder shape with larger windows.

1974

MOTORHOME

Airstream releases its first motor home, the Argosy Motorhome.

1980

AIRSTREAM
ACQUIRED FOR $1

Wade Thompson and Peter Orthwein acquire Airstream for one dollar, forming Thor Industries.

1993

VINTAGE
AIRSTREAM CLUB

As interest in the renovation and restoration of vintage Airstreams grows, WBCCI adds a new chapter, the Vintage Airstream Club. Your trailer must be twenty-five years or older to join.

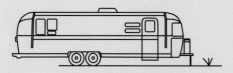

 2002

DEAM INTERIORS

The first Christopher C. Deam interiors are released, drawing a younger and more diverse buyer to Airstream.

 2005

WBCCI 50TH ANNIVERSARY

WBCCI celebrates its fiftieth anniversary.

 2006

AIRSTREAM 75TH ANNIVERSARY

The Airstream company celebrates its seventy-fifth anniversary, releasing a special edition Bambi designed by David Winick.

2010

EDDIE BAUER AIRSTREAM

The Eddie Bauer Airstream is released, with a new rear door to allow large outdoor equipment to be stored.

2015

AIRSTREAM FACTORY EXPANSION

The Airstream factory is expanded to assist with growing demand.

2016

PENDLETON TRAILER

Airstream releases the limited edition Pendleton trailer, a collaboration to pay tribute to one hundred years of the National Park Service.

2017

RETURN OF THE BASECAMP

Featuring a design influenced heavily by the original Airstream Torpedo Car Cruiser, unveiled in 2005 as a 16'2" toy-hauler, the 2017 version features a luxurious interior with an added wet bath (toilet/shower).

TOMMY BAHAMA TRAILER

Airstream releases a collaboration with a top designer, Tommy Bahama, featuring a built-in bar and ice machine!

THE CARETAKERS OF AIRSTREAM

When Wally Byam passed away, ownership of Airstream passed to his wife, Stella. Art Costello, who had worked with Wally since his days with Curtis Wright, stepped in as president of Airstream and was integral to the survival of the company.

Throughout the years Airstream had many owners and directors, but by the late 1970s things were looking very grim for the company: as gas prices soared, the trailer industry suffered. By 1979, Airstream was $12 million in debt and the company was likely to survive only another year or two at best. Fortunately, two young men could see the potential of Airstream. They could see that, with good management, Airstream would not only survive but thrive.

Wade Thompson and Peter Orthwein

Wade Thompson and Peter Orthwein had been in the business of recreational vehicles for a few years. They owned a small RV company called Hi-Lo Trailer, and had been able to see through their own experiences the changes happening in the RV industry. On August 29, 1980, Wade and Peter bought the troubled Airstream from Beatrice Foods for one dollar, forming Thor Industries—*Th* from Thompson and *or* from Orthwein.

It was a hard road, pulling Airstream back from the brink, but Wade's constant search for the best deal, and his drive to make every dollar go as far as it possibly could, saved the company. Peter recalls, "On the way to make the deal with Beatrice Foods, Wade and I were running late. We were rushing to pick up the rental car, but Wade saw the opportunity for a better deal on the rental rate—we were standing there negotiating our car rental rate as the Beatrice Foods management sat awaiting our arrival to sign on the dotted line. I must say, he did get us a good deal on the rental car!"

Wade and Peter were based in New York, but Wade spent every working day at the factory in Ohio. Through 1981, Wade shifted the way Airstream was managed, and instilled the entrepreneurial spirit in every single employee. Wade was very driven and a perfectionist, and he wouldn't accept anything less from others. He focused on the details, looked at every part of the business, and figured out how to make it more efficient and effective. Through his exceptional attention to detail and the support of Thor Industries, Airstream achieved a $1 million profit in 1981. He had turned the company around, and pulled it out of the red.

Wade stayed based at Airstream every working day for over two years, and even when he was no longer there every day he was still heavily involved in the running of Airstream. He requested a daily report noting all of the figures, which enabled him to decipher the trends in the industry and steer the company in the best direction.

Wade and Peter had a great management team that drove the Airstream company to great success over decades of ownership, including Larry Huttle, who was the president for fourteen years; Dicky Riegel in 2002; and Bob Wheeler has been the president and CEO of Airstream since 2005. All of them worked for the company for several years prior to filling the role at the top. Thor Industries still owns Airstream today.

BOB WHEELER, PRESIDENT AND CEO OF AIRSTREAM

"HE WAS A GUIDEPOST, A COMPASS, AND SHARP AS A RAZOR. WHENEVER I NEEDED TO MAKE A DECISION, I WOULD ALWAYS THINK, WHAT WOULD WADE DO?"

Wade Thompson, in his Thor costume and tie, gets a chuckle from Peter Orthwein.

Wade and Peter standing in front of one of the newly released Airstream Class A Motorhomes, 1988.

AIRSTREAM FACTORY

Wally opened the first Airstream factory in Culver City, Los Angeles, California, before the war. After World War II he reopened the factory in its new location of N. Main Street, Los Angeles. In 1952, Airstream expanded east to Jackson Center, Ohio. Airstream had factories in both California and Ohio until 1978, when the decision was made to move all operations to Jackson Center, where all Airstream trailers are being made today.

If you are even a tiny bit of an Airstream fan, you will probably want to make the pilgrimage to Jackson Center. The town has one traffic light, a population of about fifteen hundred people, and is full of the Airstream spirit. The Airstream factory lies on the main road into town, and displays some of the most famous Airstreams from the 1930s, '40s, and '50s, including Wally and Stella Byam's gold Airstream, which took part in the African caravan.

The factory offers tours, which are a great way to get up close and personal with a unique part of history. Airstreams are handcrafted, and in your tour through the factory you can see each stage in the production of these legendary trailers.

Airstreams today are still made using the basic principles conceived in the late 1930s. Today's method has been perfected with advances in technology and with Airstream's nearly ninety years of practice. Aluminum panels are riveted together to form a shell, and the speed at which these rivets are installed is pretty impressive. Two people are needed to rivet a sheet of metal—one person on either side of the sheet of aluminum, timing it perfectly, one after another. The end caps are created separately, as are the wall panels and the roof. As these five parts are riveted together, the shell takes shape. To make sure that every Airstream that leaves the factory is watertight, each trailer spends forty minutes under one hundred pounds per square inch of water pressure in a special booth.

As the factory keeps growing and changing to keep up with cutting-edge technology, high-end design, and the high demand for its trailers, you could be fooled into thinking that it is an exclusive corporate giant, but not Airstream—they are as down-to-earth as they come and welcome everyone with open arms. I highly recommend visiting the factory, even if you have to go a bit out of your way to find it!

Bob Wheeler holds up Wally Byam's creed. Its words give us all a little faith to live outside the norm and take on our own personal adventure.

BOB WHEELER, PRESIDENT AND CEO OF AIRSTREAM

"RIGHT FROM THE VERY FIRST DAY WHEN I WALKED INTO THE AIRSTREAM PLANT, I CAN REMEMBER THINKING 'THIS FEELS LIKE HOME.' YOU COULD TELL THAT PEOPLE WORKED WITH A PURPOSE. THEY HAD PRIDE IN WHAT THEY DID."

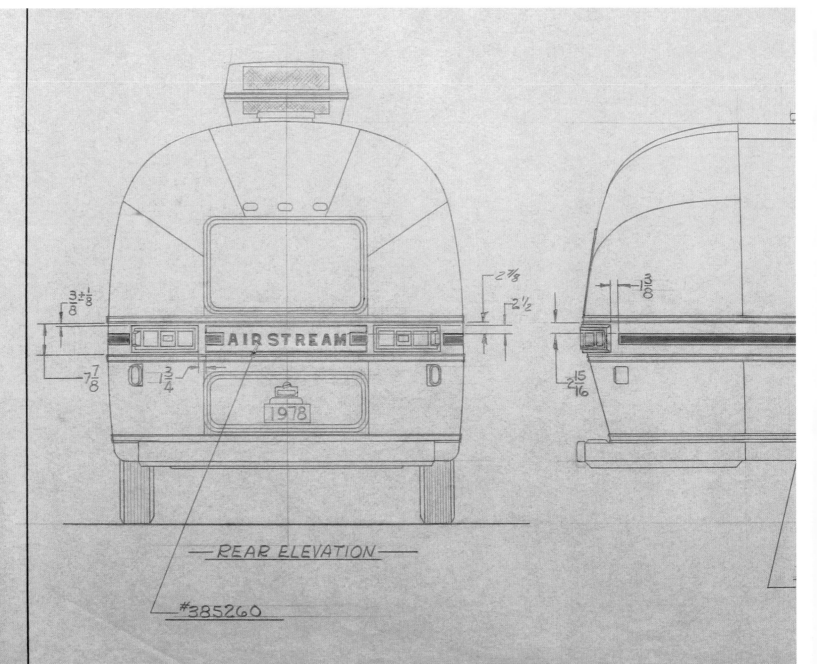

$3\frac{1}{8} \pm \frac{1}{8}$

$2\frac{7}{8}$

$2\frac{1}{2}$

AIRSTREAM

$7\frac{7}{8}$

$1\frac{3}{4}$

1978

$2\frac{15}{16}$

$3\frac{1}{16}$

—REAR ELEVATION—

#385260

AIRSTREAM INC.	DRAWN B.W.	DATE 11-22-77	CHK'D	SCALE 3/4" = 1'	PRODU AIR.

THE DESIGN OF THE AIRSTREAM

AIRSTREAM DESIGN

The legendary Airstream trailer that we know today first took its form in the mid-'30s. The Airstream Clipper was the first Airstream trailer that was made from aluminum and rivets, in its now-iconic shape, influenced by aircraft design.

During World War II, trailer designers, including Wally Byam, worked as part of the war effort to build airplanes. The skills Wally learned during this period allowed him to apply the same quality craftsmanship to his trailers. Airstream really began to find its feet in the years after the war. The company released a variety of very popular trailers, opened up additional factories to keep up with demand, and worked with the fast-moving technological advances of the age.

Driven by Wally's search for perfection, design improvements were made mid production, and each of the factories would try out different configurations, construction methods, and custom interiors. Because of this, it's very difficult to classify all the trailers made prior to the mid-'60s. Some trailer designs were never even recorded before Airstream moved on to the next featured improvement. These could be as simple as a change in cabinetry hardware, the shape of the wheel well, or the window latches. Other changes were made as a one-off or a specialty order.

After Wally passed away in 1962, the Airstream models became a little more uniform and very little customization was offered. Starting in the '70s, in-depth records of trailer models were kept, and Airstream trailer manuals were created for each model. So even though there were lots of different models and new RV designs available, these records make it easier to establish what model Airstream you own and find a manual that complements it.

The following pages are a general guide (but by no means an exhaustive catalog) to all the Airstreams ever created. For more detailed information or to find a specific model, check out the Vintage Airstream or Air Forums websites.

1930s

Torpedo

Although Wally created a variety of different trailer designs in the late 1920s, the Torpedo Car Cruiser was the first ever factory-produced Airstream. Wally sold the plans to his trailer designs, and as the business took off and demand rose, he produced kit sets and completed trailer shells. By 1931, he had opened his first factory and Torpedos were rolling out the door. By 1932, there were more than a thousand Torpedo Car Cruisers on the open road.

They were teardrop in shape, with a rounded front to deflect the oncoming wind when towed. These first trailers were made from plywood, and although the two models that followed the Torpedo were called the Silver Bullet and the Silver Cloud, neither looked anything like today's Airstream. They were made from Masonite, a steam-pressed hardboard.

In the 1930s, travel trailers were a growing commodity, and a way to access the outdoors with the comforts of modern living. The interiors were small but functional, handcrafted, and made with exceptional attention to detail. An icebox and a hand-pumped water supply stood in place of today's fridge and pressurized taps. There were no bathrooms on board, no way to hook up power and water supplies.

Clipper

William Hawley Bowlus was an aircraft builder, and during the early 1930s he turned his hand to building travel trailers. He created the Road Chief, a lightweight aluminum-based trailer in the shape of an airplane fuselage. He produced only around eighty trailers before closing his doors. Wally worked with Bowlus and was influenced by the Road Chief trailer, and he looked to produce a trailer using a similar structural form. Wally's trailer was called the Airstream Clipper, after Pan Am's Clippers, and became his first aluminum-and-rivets trailer.

He created a prototype in 1936 that went through various iterations before he settled on a design and released it for mass manufacture in 1937. At nineteen feet long, the Airstream Clipper fulfilled the dream of a lightweight travel trailer that would tow beautifully, given its semi-monocoque structure and rounded fuselage shape.

The interior was made of laminated wooden panels, cut in the same shape as the exterior aluminum panels. Combined with quality furnishings, the Clipper featured one of the most luxurious early Airstream interiors.

1940s

During World War II, aluminum for aircrafts was in high demand. The government outlawed aluminum for use on recreational trailers. Wally shut up the Airstream shop in 1942 and, along with many of his employees, found work in the aircraft industry. He worked for Curtis Wright's aircraft company for several years, where he learned many skills that would enable him to perfect the Airstream trailer structure.

In 1946, when the war was over, Wally and Curtis Wright combined their knowledge and skills to start building travel trailers. During this brief merger, the Curtis Wright Clipper was born. It was based on Airstream's 1937 Clipper, but improved with aircraft-manufacturing techniques and aircraft materials such as aluminum alloy and insulation, as well as high-quality tools and aircraft construction techniques. In 1947, Wally decided to go back to working for himself and reopened Airstream.

Wally went on to design a range of new Airstream travel trailers, and later that year the Airstream Liner was released. The exterior resembled the Airstream Clipper's 1930s art deco style, with a large oval-window front and back. It also had a single stoplight on the rear (before that became illegal in 1948). In the late '40s, Wally also invented the "door-within-a-door" featured on some models, so that you were able to have a door open to let the wind through, but have an insect screen behind it. This screen-door design carried throughout the early '50s.

David Winick's 1948 Wee Wind restoration, featuring a door-within-a-door design. David took this rare, iconic trailer back to its bare bones, painstakingly restoring and repairing every aspect, as well as adding a high-end, stunning interior.

Pipe Chassis

To make the trailers lightweight, Wally invented a unique chassis that utilized a single-pipe frame support running from the back of the trailer through to the front to form the trailer hitch. The cross members lay across this to support the weight. This pipe chassis was inspired by the mule-drawn wagon in which Wally had spent so much time in as a young child.

WALLY BYAM

"THUS TODAY'S AIRSTREAM IS MORE AIRPLANE THAN TRAILER. IT IS BUILT ON AIRPLANE JIGS, WITH AIRPLANE TECHNIQUES, USING AIRPLANE ALUMINUM ALLOYS, AND WITH AIRPLANE INSULATION. IT IS LIGHT ENOUGH AND STRONG ENOUGH TO FLY, BUT STILL HAS THE RELIABLE COVERED-WAGON UNDERCARRIAGE."

Light and Aerodynamic

To continue proving how lightweight the Airstream travel trailers were, Wally invited Alfred Letourneur, a French cyclist renowned for breaking the world speed record on a bicycle, to pull a 1947 Airstream Liner. Photographs of Letourneur pulling the Liner were a great marketing tool, and ended up becoming the Airstream logo for many years.

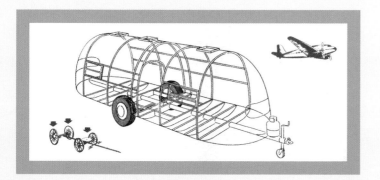

THE STRUCTURE OF AN AIRSTREAM

Aluminum and Rivets

Airstreams were originally produced with the same aluminum that was sourced to make aircrafts. Throughout the years, the aluminum composites that Airstream uses have changed with advances in technology. Even in the early days, all Airstream trailers coming off the factory line had a protective coating applied to the aluminum. Customers had to make a special request for it to come with a mirror shine. Today the mirror shine is particularly coveted on vintage trailers, although it requires a lot of work and upkeep.

Trailers made before the mid-'90s can be polished up to a mirror shine with some work. The ability to bring an Airstream to a mirror shine doesn't have to do with the type of aluminum used, but with the ability to remove the clear, protective coating. By the late 1990s, Airstream was applying a particularly sturdy clear coat that is near impossible to remove. It ensures the aluminum stays protected but also means you will likely be unable to achieve a mirror shine on a late-model Airstream.

Framework

The basic principle of the shell and its frame has been the same since the Clipper in the 1930s. There have been changes in patterns and shapes, but the semi-monocoque structure of the Airstream has sustained throughout the years. The semi-monocoque structure relies on the external skin for strength, and therefore the framing could be lightweight and more of a guiding structure for the external panels. The rounded shape enabled the wind to pass by at great speeds without creating drag or undue side-wind pressures. Both the exterior aluminum skin and the interior aluminum skin absorb most of the loads applied to the Airstream.

This is important to understand if you are renovating an Airstream and intend to take off the interior aluminum panels to access the insulation or wiring. They are part of the structure too, and removing them compromises the structure's strength. This is okay if you are in a workshop with a controlled environment and the Airstream isn't mobile. But moving the Airstream in this state—or leaving it in the elements, exposed to strong wind, rain, or snow—could crumple the structure.

Wally's first chassis was the pipe chassis, but by the early '50s, Airstream had moved to a ladder frame. The design of the frame did vary from the California factories to the Ohio factory, but the principle was the same. Airstream has stayed with this ladder frame since the '50s, updating throughout the years with the technology of the time. The axle construction method made a giant leap forward in the early '60s, introducing the DuraTorque axle, made from a rubber core, which dramatically reduced the impact of traveling on the open road.

The flooring is laid on top of the chassis, and the shell is attached to the floor and chassis. Throughout the years this connection has changed slightly, and in the '70s a new installation method led to a few trailers suffering floor separation which caused leaks and floor rot. In the 1980s, this was rectified through an ingenious U-shaped channel that sealed the flooring from the elements.

To protect the bottom of the Airstream, and also to install and protect insulation in the floor, each Airstream has a "belly pan." This belly pan encompasses the underside of the chassis, wrapping up to be riveted onto the bottom edge of the shell. This belly pan does a great job of protecting the underside of an Airstream, but does make it very difficult to reach the chassis for any repairs. And if your vintage Airstream called a paddock "home" for the last few years, it more than likely made a nice warm spot for rodents to also call home.

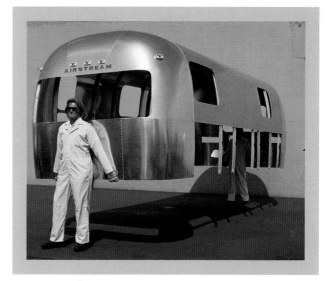

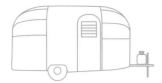

1950s

The early '50s brought change in design but also substantial variation throughout the Airstream trailer range. In 1952, Airstream opened a second factory in Ohio. With the factories varying slightly in the Airstream designs they produced—and the rate at which they changed and/or upgraded those designs—there were large variations in Airstreams produced in the same year and at the same size specifications.

The early '50s introduced a new framework for the chassis: the box beam ladder frame with an A-shaped hitch. The body also changed, becoming substantially squarer with flatter walls and new flat windows, though for a time you could get the flatter front window paired with the rounder 1940s oval-window tail, which made for quite an interesting body shape.

The flatter ends required a tighter compound curve of the end caps. This new end cap design consisted of thirteen pie-shaped pieces of aircraft-grade aluminum that were riveted together to form the shape. Because of the minimal flexibility of the aluminum, the end caps required these thirteen pieces to be able to form a tight curve and create a reliable seal between each panel.

In 1954, the tail changed from sitting pretty much vertically to having a slightly sloping tail end. Additionally, Airstream introduced a unique tail design believed to be made only in California, the whale tail—or as it was sometimes referred to,

the Dutchman's cap. Instead of thirteen panels, the whale tail consisted of nine panels: four panels wrapped horizontally on each side and a center piece attached to the roof panel, running down and flaring out to the top of the window. It is thought that this was introduced to save labor, as riveting thirteen panels together was very time-consuming, but now whale tails are quite the collector's item.

By 1957, a new stretch-forming technology enabled the manipulation of the aluminum panels, and by curving them slightly Airstream was able to reduce the thirteen panels to just seven.

The year 1957 also brought an advancement in the interiors, when Airstream released the International—the first ever "self-contained" travel trailer. It freed the user from hookups and allowed adventurers to venture beyond RV parks.

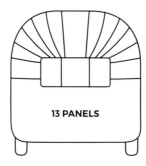

13 PANELS

WHALE TAIL

The renovation of this stunning 1955 Flying Cloud, featuring a whale tail (or the Dutchman's cap), is the creation of Paul and Mary Drag. The hard work speaks for itself—this trailer is one of the most outstanding you will ever see. The attention to detail is exquisite, and the thoughtfulness behind every design feature is truly evident.

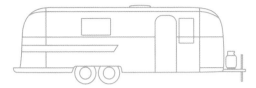

1960s

Between 1957 and 1964, the body and shape of the Airstream remained relatively consistent. The only major changes were new-style windows that were released in 1959 and a new-style axle in 1961, switching from the leaf springs to the DuraTorque axle, which offered a major upgrade in the suspension system.

In the early '60s, Airstream released two extremes in length of Airstream models. In 1961, the legendary Bambi was born, a self-contained Airstream in a small sixteen-foot package. The following year, in 1962, the Western Pacific trailer was released, a massive forty-foot trailer that featured two doors. They were not made to travel on the road but to offer housing to crews working on the Western Pacific Railroad far away from civilization.

In 1964, the end cap panels changed once again, introducing only five panels, which is still the configuration of today's Airstreams.

This beautiful example of a 1968 Airstream Trade Wind, with the newly introduced five panels, was renovated by ARC Airstream. The gorgeous interior is featured in the next chapter, on page 64.

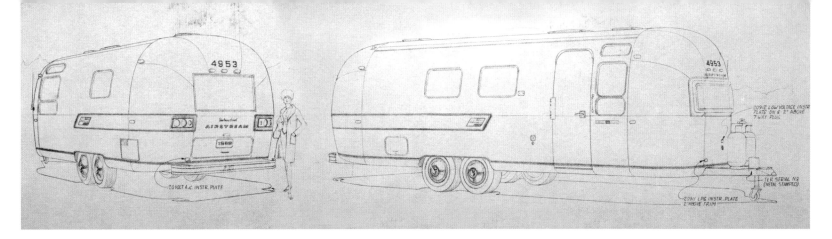

The New Body of 1969

In 1969, the body shape experienced a major change. Each Airstream became longer by a foot and wider by four inches. The overall silhouette became a lot rounder in both the front and back. The company also introduced bigger, wider windows, especially in the living area, where side windows were added to make three windows across the front.

AIRSTREAM SPECS

Airstream Widths

In the '40s and early '50s, Airstreams were released in a variety of widths. Some were 6'6" and others were up to 7'6", though on average they measured seven feet wide. In 1951, the width became uniform at 7'4". The year 1959 brought 7'7" trailers, although the Bambi was released at seven feet. The 1969 trailer width increased to almost eight feet, and in 1994, it grew again to 8'5.5". Airstreams are still released in this width today, although trailers released outside of the United States range from 7'6" to 8'2", given the smaller roads, different parking, and legal requirements.

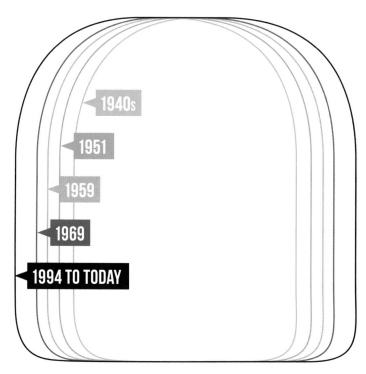

1940s
1951
1959
1969
1994 TO TODAY

WIDTH IN FEET AND INCHES: 7' 7'4" 7'7" 8' **8'5.5"**

Airstream Names

Early on, Wally named his Airstreams after the aircraft industry, which he had been so heavily involved with and which had greatly influenced his design methods. The Clipper, his first aluminum-and-rivets trailer, was named after Pan Am Clippers. After the war, he named his trailers after different types of wind, thought to be influenced by his time as a marine. Names like Trade Wind were added to the Airstream trailer collective.

In the beginning, names of Airstream models indicated their length. A new name would be introduced to indicate a different size. During the '60s, names could also refer to an upgrade on systems and interior, like the Land Yacht and International. In the '80s, model names began to indicate only the quality of services and fittings, and a single model would be offered in a variety of lengths. For example, the Caravelle came in twenty-, twenty-two-, and twenty-four-foot models, and the Excella II in twenty-five-, twenty-eight-, and thirty-one-foot models. This is still true today; for example, a Flying Cloud comes in lengths ranging from 19'2" through 30'11".

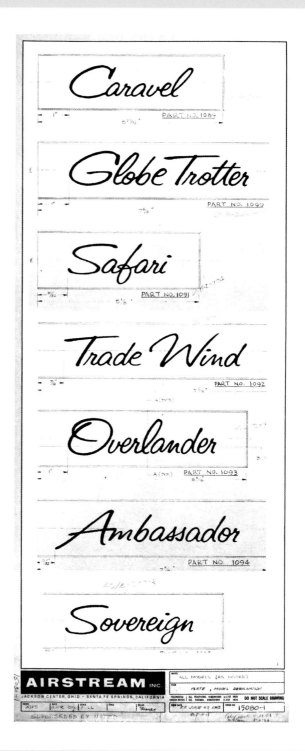

Airstream Lengths

This is by no means a complete list of models, but this graph provides a general idea of models that were released over the years and their lengths. Measurements give the length from the hitch to the tail, not just the body of the Airstream.

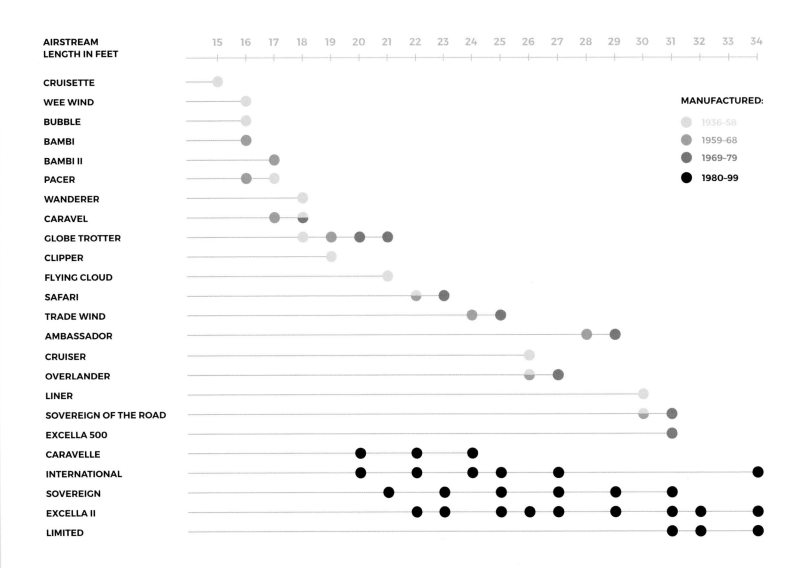

AIRSTREAM LENGTH IN FEET

15 16 17 18 19 20 21 22 23 24 25 26 27 28 29 30 31 32 33 34

CRUISETTE
WEE WIND
BUBBLE
BAMBI
BAMBI II
PACER
WANDERER
CARAVEL
GLOBE TROTTER
CLIPPER
FLYING CLOUD
SAFARI
TRADE WIND
AMBASSADOR
CRUISER
OVERLANDER
LINER
SOVEREIGN OF THE ROAD
EXCELLA 500
CARAVELLE
INTERNATIONAL
SOVEREIGN
EXCELLA II
LIMITED

MANUFACTURED:

1936–58
1959–68
1969–79
1980–99

Floor Plans

Airstreams from all eras have three main layout variables: length, bathroom placement (central or rear), and sleeping configuration. Here are some examples of Airstream floor layouts from the '70s.

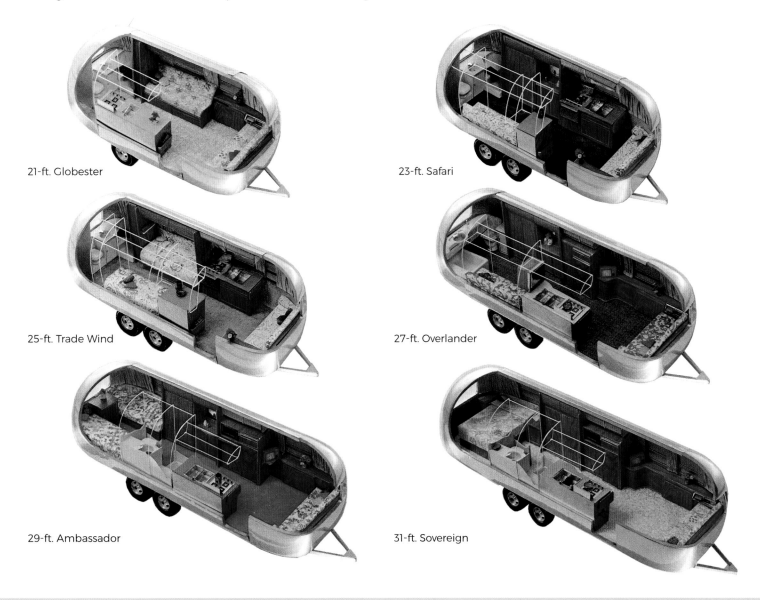

21-ft. Globester

23-ft. Safari

25-ft. Trade Wind

27-ft. Overlander

29-ft. Ambassador

31-ft. Sovereign

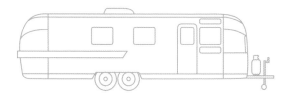

1970s

The "new body" introduced in 1969 would not change throughout the '70s. Not only was the design different but the new trailers were also manufactured differently from early '60s trailers. Previously, the way in which the shell was attached to the chassis was effective at keeping the rain out, but it was also time-consuming to make. In the '70s, the decision was made to attach the shell in a different way and in some trailers led to separation of the frame over time that allowed rain to rot the floor and rust the chassis.

The interior style changed dramatically, with the introduction of fiberglass interior end caps and lightweight interior cabinetry made from aluminum framing and veneer panels, which replaced the solid-wood interiors of the '60s.

Trailers built prior to 1974 featured only one waste tank to catch the black water (sewage). Prior to this time, it was legal to dump gray water (used water from the shower and sink) at your camping site, whereas today it is not permitted. After 1974, Airstreams featured both a black and gray tank. Therefore, if you are looking to buy anything manufactured prior to 1974, you will need to install a gray water tank, or some method of catching the water externally. There are small tank designs especially made to fit between the cross-members of the chassis, which, although a bit tricky to install, require very little alteration to the structure. Alternatively, as many professional designers do, you can do a complete redesign and rebuild of the chassis to allow larger tanks to be installed.

This original '70s Airstream is situated in Malibu, as an accommodation offered by Murray and Kay, as featured on page 150. Book Airstream Vintage Trailer Adventure on AirBnB.

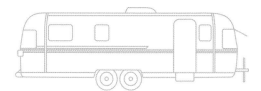

Argosy

In 1972, Airstream released a new design called the Argosy, nicknamed the "Painted Airstream." They were a cheaper option compared to their shiny Airstream counterpart as they used a one-piece steel end cap instead of the aluminum panels. They were also used to test out new features, and if they were a success they were incorporated into Airstream trailers. A great example is the large panoramic windows, featured here on Melanie and Damien's Argosy trailer, Twinkie.

Many Argosy owners today take the Painted Airstream to the extreme, painting it orange, red, or pink, or even using it as a canvas for a mural. Chad and Cate, inspired by Woody Guthrie's song "This Land Is Your Land," hand painted this stunning mural on their 1976 twenty-two-foot Argosy. The interior is just as spectacular, check it out on their instagram page @argosyodyssey.

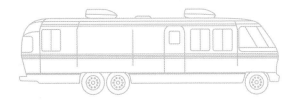

Motorhome

The Motorhome also became a staple in the Airstream range in the '70s, initially with the release of the Argosy Motorhome, which was in production between 1974 and 1979. The Argosy Motorhome was released in a variety of sizes, including a tiny twenty-foot Motorhome. These are in high demand today, and some owners have stripped the paint to reveal the mostly silver body, although the dark-colored steel end caps are often quite obvious. In 1979 and through the 1980s, Airstream Class A Motorhomes were released, which were similar to the Airstream trailers, featuring shiny aluminum. In 1979, the company released twenty-four- and twenty-eight-foot models, but during the '80s longer lengths were released, ranging up to thirty-seven feet.

This beautiful example of a twenty-foot Argosy Motorhome has been released as a cute bus.

This original Motorhome is owned by Adam and Susan Maffei. These photos were taken when they first acquired it, before their restorations had begun.

This stunning renovation of an Airstream Motorhome was created by professional Airstream designers American Retro Caravans. More of their beautiful work is featured in the Airstream Designers chapter, on page 62.

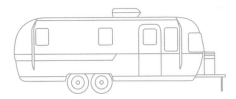

1980s

New ownership by Thor Industries brought new life back into Airstream, and the company focused on listening to customers and providing quality and durability. In the first year of Thor's management, there were substantial changes to the manufacturing techniques, bringing quality back into the product. You can still see this today, as Airstreams from this period, while considered vintage, have stood the test of time.

The '80s became an era of bigger is better, and in 1982, a thirty-four-foot three-axle trailer made its debut—the largest Airstream trailer to go into mass production. This also meant that smaller trailers were dropped from the sales catalog. The smallest size trailer you could get in 1982 was twenty-seven feet. In 1985, Airstream introduced a twenty-five-footer, and in 1987, a twenty-three-footer was brought to the market, but just for a short time: only fifty were ever made. The appeal of not having a dedicated bedroom didn't fit within the '80s marketplace.

By the late '80s, Airstream had firmly found its feet again, and a variety of different models began to fill the market, including a range of fiberglass motor homes that looked nothing like the silver aluminum-and-rivets trailers. You wouldn't have been able to tell they were Airstreams if it were not for the top quality with which they were produced. Some consumers loved them and some Airstream aficionados snubbed them, but they were all part of the growing process for Airstream.

This stunning and very rare 1987 twenty-three-foot Sovereign is owned by Vintage Airstream Club president Iain Cameron.

From the left, the 1988 Airstream Land Yacht (Square Stream) and the Airstream 5th Wheeler. Not many of these were ever created, and they are quite the collector's item these days.

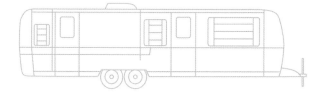

"Square Stream"

In 1986, Argosy became a testing ground again as Airstream released a very rectangular-shaped Argosy trailer. It was made from bonded aluminum and painted beige. By 1988, it had been removed from the Airstream lineup, but in 1989, the design reappeared as the Airstream Land Yacht, this time painted silver with a baked enamel finish. The design got nicknamed the "Square Stream" and although at the time it wasn't very popular among Airstream aficionados, today they have a dedicated following.

Argosy Trailer (Square Stream) with the bonded aluminum and beige paint.

1990s

In 1994, the Airstream trailer had its first major change since 1969. Although the general bullet shape was kept, the body became squarer, and some of the thirty-four-foot wide-body Excella and Limited models became wide bodies at 8.5' wide. By 1996, all models had become wide bodies. All Airstreams produced today have bodies with this same shape and width.

In the late '90s, the market was changing: those who loved Airstream in the '50s and '60s, in Airstream's heyday, were now in their later years, and Airstream wanted to reach out to a younger generation. The Safari was introduced, and at twenty-five feet it was lightweight and could be towed by an SUV or powerful car. It was also cheaper, costing about 20 percent less than some of its contemporaries. This made Airstream more accessible, and it once again gained pop culture status.

CHRISTOPHER DEAM

Christopher Deam

At the end of the '90s, an architect named Christopher Deam shook up the Airstream company. Wally Byam had viewed the Airstream like a TARDIS from home, so no matter where you were, even in the middle of an African desert, you could step into your trailer and be home. There was no intention for the interior to reflect the exterior design-wise, but as time went on, the disconnect between the two became obvious to the younger generations.

Christopher Deam set about creating an "interior that fulfilled the promise of the exterior." In 2002, his CCD International Bambi was released. They were very popular and introduced an entirely different group of people to the RV market.

"THE SHELL WAS ORIGINALLY CONCEIVED AS A LIGHTWEIGHT, MODERN, FUTURISTIC, HIGH-TECH POD FOR HURTLING DOWN THE FREEWAY, BUT THE INTERIOR WAS COMPLETELY OUT OF SYNC WITH THAT."

VIEW ONLINE

CDEAM.COM

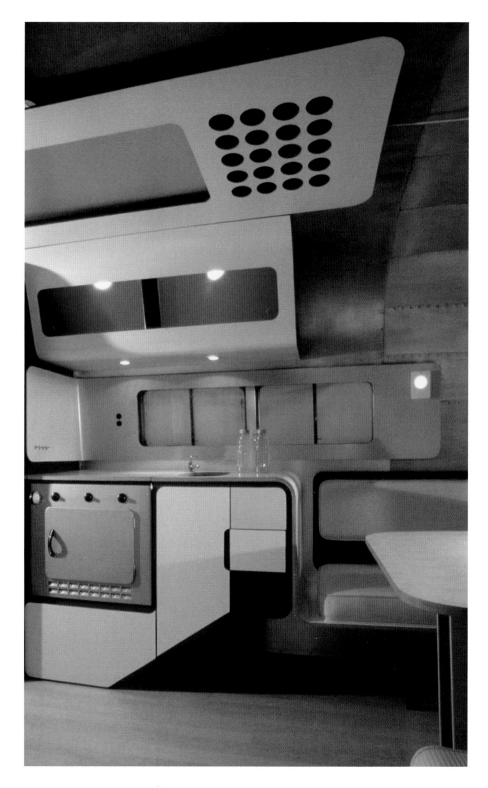

Christopher Deam got the attention of Dicky Riegel and Wade Thompson with this exquisite prototype trailer. Intending to showcase Wilsonart laminate, Christopher used this material to give a fresh look to the interior of the Airstream. This design influenced the first collaboration with Airstream and Deam, the CCD Interational Series.

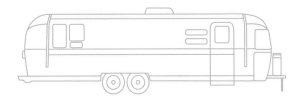

2000s

Airstream was gaining new audiences and becoming popular throughout the generations. The introduction of new interior designs helped to solidify Airstream once again as a company on the cutting edge of modern design. The 2000s were a fresh start for Airstream. With the new CCD designs, Airstream had discovered the benefits of collaborating with outside designers and established brands.

Airstream's Seventy-fifth Anniversary

The seventy-fifth anniversary of Airstream was a unique opportunity to do something really different. Airstream collaborated with renowned custom Airstream trailer designer David Winick. Winick's trailers had caught the eyes of many celebrities and design aficionados. His limited edition 75th Anniversary Bambi Airstream (only seventy-five were made) were sold out before they had even been manufactured.

The exquisite interior of the 75th Anniversary Bambi, designed by David Winick. Opposite page: David Winick's customized door screen.

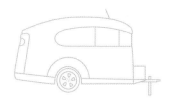

Basecamp

In 2005, Airstream, in collaboration with Nissan, introduced the smallest Airstream trailer in recent years, the Basecamp. The design echoed back to early Airstreams, mimicking the shape of the Torpedo Car Cruiser of 1931. The interior was functional, allowing space for active adventurers to store their toys. At 16'2" long, it had room for your motorbike, Jet Ski, or any other toy that took your fancy. The Basecamp was one of the smallest toy-hauler trailers ever made. 2017 brings the re-release of this beautiful little Airstream with a luxurious interior and a newly featured wet bath (toilet/shower).

1931

2017

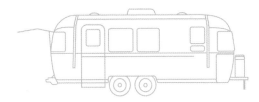

Toy Haulers and Limited Edition Trailers

Airstream toy haulers went from small to super large with the release of a thirty-four-foot trailer/toy hauler called the PanAmerica. The rear end of the trailer opened up to reveal a twelve-foot garage at the tail of the trailer to store your toys, with the living quarters up in the front. A customized version of the PanAmerica created in collaboration with Victorinox Swiss Army toured the country to celebrate the 125th anniversary of the Swiss Army Knife and the release of the nineteen-foot Victorinox Swiss Army Special Edition Airstream.

The rear-door style of the PanAmerica trailer was a hit, and became the precursor to the Eddie Bauer Airstream, a collaboration with the legendary clothing brand. The Eddie Bauer Airstream featured the PanAmerica-style rear door that opened up to the dining area. The dining table could be removed while traveling so you could load in long recreational equipment, kayaks, bicycles, even a motorbike if you so wished.

In 2016, using a similar trailer configuration, Airstream joined forces with another big brand, Pendleton, for the National Park Service centennial, releasing one hundred Pendleton Limited Edition trailers with Pendleton decor, stunning leather seats, and decorated paneling. 2017 sees the release of the Tommy Bahama collaboration, set up for luxurious outdoor living. Fantastic prints by Tommy Bahama are combined with luxury essentials like a built-in bar and ice machine!

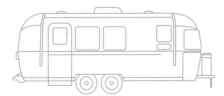

2010s

Airstream's popularity has become undeniable; the amount of trailers rolling off the lot in Jackson Center throughout the recent years is testament to its iconic status. As ever, the technology is constantly being updated. For instance, Quietstream Air Conditioning offers ducted cooling with significantly reduced noise compared with the traditional RV A/C units. The beautiful interiors are personalized by their owners just like their vintage counterparts, showcasing the wondering spirit of their residents.

The Vintages, an Airstream accommodation in the heart of Oregon's wine country, feature their personal touch to this modern Airstream. Details on The Vintages can be found on page 151.

A little beauty called Poppy, this Caravel's interior was created by ARC Airstreams.

DESIGNING YOUR OWN AIRSTREAM

WITH A DESIGNER

PROFESSIONAL DESIGNERS

The beautiful thing about Airstreams is that they are exactly what Wally envisaged them to be: a way to go adventuring through the world while taking the comforts of home with you. What makes Airstreams as popular today as they were in the 1930s is not only the wonderful engineering but also the timeless design.

Because of their design and materials, Airstreams really are a blank canvas for anyone to add their own unique personality to. You can choose quality over quantity, sentimentality over mainstream, and personal practicalities over having to suit everyone else. This is what makes Airstreams so unique, and it's also why people flock to your door when you pull your Airstream into a campsite. You will get used to total strangers being fascinated by your home on wheels, and having them want to take a quick look inside.

Creating your personalized home on wheels can be a daunting project. But professional designers make this process easy for you: you get to create the trailer that you've always dreamed of, while leaving it to the professionals to handle the practicalities and the safety issues. Most designers do charge a pretty penny for this service, but you can be assured that your Airstream will be like new compared to its vintage counterpart.

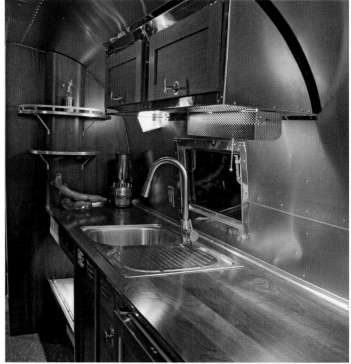

David Winick is one of the original professional designers of custom Airstreams. His passion for high quality and exquisite detail has received the attention of many high-end clients, including the Airstream company itself. To the right is a 1950 Cruiser interior immaculately designed and built by David; more about David and his designs on page 67.

TOP 6 — DESIGN CONSIDERATIONS FROM THE PROFESSIONALS

Professional designers all have a very similar design process—and will endeavor to learn the answers to the following questions before they begin a project. Whether you enlist a professional or do the hard yards yourself, answering these questions will get your design project off to a great start.

1

How do you plan on using the trailer? Is it going to be a guesthouse parked on your land, a holiday getaway, or a full-time traveling home?

2

When you travel, do you want to be self-contained (boondock relying on solar or generator power, and tanked water) or use full hookups?

3

How many people will you be traveling with? What kind of sleeping arrangements do you need? Do you mind a bed that you have to fold out and set up every night? Or do you want a permanent bed?

4

What are the sleeping arrangements for children or extra guests? Do you need a dinette to convert? A foldout couch (gaucho)?

5

What kind of systems do you need? Electric? Water? Plumbing? Solar? Gas?

6

What's your design inspiration? A photograph, a memento, a memory, a piece of fabric, or just something that makes you smile?

"EVERYONE IS BROUGHT TOGETHER BY THE ONE LOVE OF THE AIRSTREAM, BUT ON THE INSIDE EVERYONE CAN BE THEMSELVES. IT'S AN ESCAPE POD, AND IT CAN ALSO BE A DEEPLY PERSONAL SPACE."

ARC AIRSTREAMS

ARC (American Retro Caravans) is based in the beautiful English countryside in a spot that you would almost certainly drive past if it weren't for the spot of silver catching the sun through the trees. It is a unique little hideaway in Somerset filled with Airstreams from all eras, crafted into stunning original designs. This small family-run business was started by Kathy Morrison and Darren Perry in 2008, importing vintage Airstreams and renovating the interiors for the European market.

Darren started his career in sheet metal work, carpentry, and joinery, and Kathy has many years' experience in the fashion and design industry, with an eye for stunning interior design. Combining these skill sets was the perfect start for ARC. They now have a growing team to help keep up with demand and create an array of high-end designs in a variety of different Airstream trailers—each with beautiful personal touches to suit the clients' needs.

VIEW ONLINE

ARCAIRSTREAMS.CO.UK

Ralph Lauren–Inspired

"The Airstream chosen for this project was a 1964 Airstream Overlander," Kathy recalls, "The design brief was a country feel while also being luxurious, and Ralph Lauren's Corral Canyon seemed to fit the bill. We wanted an American-outdoors feel, an interior that embraced the origins of the Airstream, a feeling of the great outdoors and the open plains of the Wild West. The Airstream can sleep four and is fully centrally heated with A/C, a surround-sound system, two TVs, an oven, cooktop, fridge, walk-in shower, toilet, and basin."

Huntsman

"We were asked by Pierre Lagrange from the famous Huntsman Savile Row tailors to design two interiors for extra accommodation for hunting parties at his country estate. The Airstreams were two 1960s Airstream Trade Winds, a 1965 and a 1968," Kathy describes. "The interiors were inspired by hunting lodges and included walls lined with Huntsman tweed. We used antler handles, distressed wood, and dark-painted walls to create a hunting-lodge feel. These Airstreams boasted an emperor-sized bed and luxury walk-in bathroom." The exterior for this beautiful Airstream is featured in the '60s Airstream Design section, on page 40.

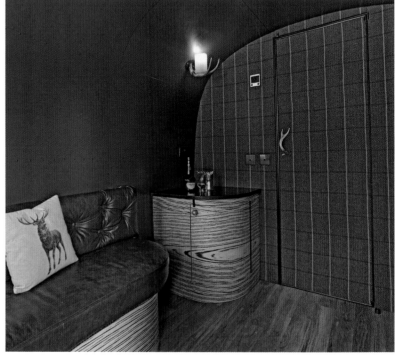

Design Tips from ARC

When starting the design for your floor plan, chalk it out, to size, on the floor of your Airstream. It gives you a much better concept of space before you get into drawing scaled floor plans and producing 3-D models.

Nine times out of ten, clients like to have the bathroom in the center, mainly because rear bathrooms in a vintage trailer make the shower quite narrow, low, and awkward. As well as this, while sitting in your trailer, being able to see from one end of the trailer to the other creates a great sense of space, whereas inserting a rear bath cuts off the end of the trailer, making a small space even smaller.

No matter how good your ventilation, your Airstream will always have more condensation than a house would; therefore real, untreated timbers will warp and move. Veneers are a good alternative.

KATHY MORRISON

"IN A SMALL SPACE, MORE THAN THREE STRONG COLORS CAN GET A BIT BONKERS, BUT THEN AGAIN SOMETIMES PEOPLE WANT BONKERS!"

European-Specific Tips

In the UK and Europe, try not to go past twenty-six feet in length. Given the sizes of European roads, having a trailer any bigger makes it very difficult to tow and takes the fun out of it!

Maximum legal width in the UK is 2.5 meters (8.2 feet). With most American Airstreams being currently released at sizes just over this, you need to choose vintage or a new Airstream specifically made for the European market.

"I FOCUS ON THE DETAILS. YOU CAN CREATE DETAILS THAT DON'T COST THAT MUCH MONEY BUT MAKE ALL THE DIFFERENCE TO A DESIGN, MAKING IT MORE PERSONAL AND ATTRACTIVE."

DAVID WINICK

David Winick is an outstanding craftsman with excellent spatial awareness and an eye for beautiful design. His unique design style is recognizable from the beautiful spectrum of materials he employs to the way in which he uses space and light to create a masterful interior.

He bought his first Airstream in 2002 on eBay, a 1968 Airstream Trade Wind in "relatively good" condition. David kept the trailer for over a year before deciding that it needed some "light maintenance." Once the Airstream was in his workshop, his imagination started to spin, and before he knew it, he was in the middle of a full renovation. "It was so much fun I couldn't wait to get out to my shop every morning," David recalls.

Working as a custom metalworker and joiner for many years, he had built up the skills and the talent to tackle one of the hardest interior spaces. Given Airstream's compound curves and the shifting and moving of each individual piece of the trailer over the years, no two trailers are ever exactly alike. As a master craftsman, with a focus on detail and a very fine eye for perfection, he designs trailers into works of art.

For David, the key to good design of small spaces is to first consider and maximize the use of space, making a space really flexible, and considering how you would be able to move and function within that space. With an overall aim to keep weight to a minimum, David chooses very carefully the materials he uses, but always makes sure he uses "honest materials": real wood, beautiful choices in metals, and well-designed feature pieces that add another level to the design.

There is no such thing as a rush job with David. He wants to produce the perfect trailer every time, and that takes dedication. No wonder he has a star-studded following—James Hetfield, Anthony Kiedis, and Patrick Dempsey all own David Winick Airstream trailers.

VIEW ONLINE

VINTAGETRAILERING.COM

This 1958 Flying Cloud was originally built in California. (The wheel arches feature a slight slant—this design feature was only ever released through the California factory.) This exquisite interior (right) was designed specifically for the client by David, featuring his trademark metalwork, beautiful textures and fabrics, and gorgeous materials.

Below is a 1950 Cruiser, another example of his impeccable restorations.

"COMING FROM AN ARCHITECTURE BACKGROUND, WE UNDERSTAND DESIGN, HARMONY, BALANCE, AND SCALE: VALUABLE ASSETS IN THE DESIGN OF SMALL SPACES."

HOFMANN ARCHITECTURE

Matthew Hofmann took a little bit of a gamble in 2009, quitting his job during the middle of a recession to renovate an Airstream trailer. He had a dream to build his own business by working and living simply on the Californian coast. With a bit of a tentative "good luck" wished by friends and family, he bought a 1978 Excella and began to create himself a new home office. The process definitely had a few learning curves. Although Matthew has a background in construction and is a licensed architect, learning the particulars of how plumbing installation works in a trailer was a bit of a challenge. But with an exquisite eye for design and a true understanding of how living spaces interrelate, Matthew built a home office that became an internet sensation.

Word spread about Matthew's Airstream trailer—his new approach to the Airstream interior was a hit. The timing also couldn't have been better, as in the following years there was a resurgence of passion for these shiny aluminum trailers. It was 2011 and the economic tide was turning, but many had learned a lesson in the 2008 downturn. Living big isn't all it's cracked up to be, and could end up leaving you very vulnerable. The story of how Matthew was living a wonderful life in a beautifully designed luxury Airstream trailer was an inspiration to many.

Matthew's phone started to ring with people who wanted his help; they wanted him to design a trailer that they could live the good life in. With an interior style that is full of light, featuring beautiful materials and simple color palettes, Hofarc (Hofmann Architecture) had found a niche. Today Matthew has a fantastic team working with him, including his dad, Wally Hofmann, in a great workshop in Santa Barbara. They produce one-of-a-kind designs, and aren't afraid to push the boundaries and offer clients something a little outside the box.

VIEW ONLINE

HOFARC.COM

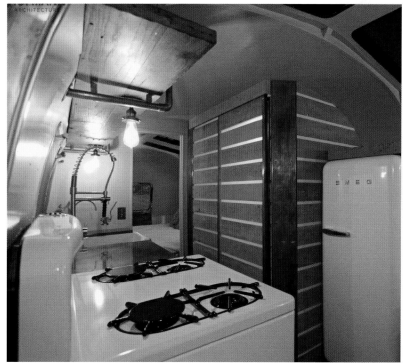

This 1974 thirty-one-foot Sovereign, nicknamed "Elizabeth," is a stunning restoration featuring twelve skylights, and an extra-special rear door, opening up the bedroom to the beautiful view from its new home in the Sonoma Valley.

"AIRSTREAM ARE OUR PARTNERS; THEY KNOW WE WILL PROTECT THEIR BRAND AS MUCH AS OUR OWN."

TIMELESS TRAVEL TRAILERS

Creating luxury Airstream travel trailers came as second nature to Brett Hall. He had previously been producing interiors of luxury passenger railcars in Denver, Colorado, but when the rail company shifted to Portland, he started a specialty construction company, working with architects who thought outside the box to create unique items for their builds. One of the architects brought Brett her vintage Airstream and asked him to make it into a mobile office for her. When others saw the end result, they started asking, "Do you have any more of those trailers?" That was in 2004, and by 2006, Timeless Travel Trailers was exclusively building luxury travel trailers.

Timeless Travel Trailers has a wonderful relationship with Airstream and is authorized by Airstream to use a new shell and outfit it to a client's needs. Each year, Timeless designs fifteen to twenty new-shell trailers, including a lot of commercial builds as well as on-location trailers for Hollywood stars. The majority of the company's business is vintage Airstreams, customizing interiors to suit clientele and renovating trailer shells from the ground up.

Timeless converts Airstreams for both commercial and mobile home use, and the style is varied to suit the customers' requirements. With a wealth of experience, Timeless is not afraid to tackle projects that are a little bit on the extreme end of what a mobile home traditionally is. Whether it's building forty-foot trailers or sixteen-thousand-pound trailers, Timeless has done it all.

VIEW ONLINE

TIMELESSTRAVELTRAILERS.COM

This 1971 Sovereign—nicknamed Stardust, Montana—is rustic and comfortable in style, but with contemporary fittings and finishes. With the predominant material being timber, a colored stain creates a beautiful layering of shapes and spaces.

"WE TRY TO CAPTURE THE FEELING OF THE ERA, USING AUTHENTIC MATERIALS AND TEXTURES THAT WERE UTILIZED IN THAT ERA, RATHER THAN CREATING SOMETHING THAT FEATURES TODAY'S VERSION OF THAT ERA."

FLYTE CAMP

Justin and Anna Scribner have always had a passion for vintage: cars, trailers, motorcycles, appliances—you name it, they were obsessed. Restoring vintage trailers grew into a hobby for the couple after they purchased their first trailer in 1998. Justin worked in construction and Anna as a designer—by combining their skills they decided to renovate a 1964 Airstream to take their son camping and relive some of their own childhood memories. But in 2008 the recession hit, and to weather the storm, they sadly had to sell much of their vintage collection, including the 1964 Airstream. Knowing how upset Anna was to lose their family trailer, Justin headed out the very next day and bought another vintage trailer to renovate. It was in rough shape, but by spending every moment he had in the driveway of their home, renovating and rebuilding, he had soon created a "new" vintage trailer. The recession was still having a great impact on Bend, Oregon, and construction jobs were becoming few and far between, so they decided to put that one up for sale also.

To keep themselves afloat they decided to buy yet another trailer to renovate and sell, but winter was coming and Justin couldn't keep working in the driveway, so they decided to rent out one of the many vacant shops in the area. During the next six months, they tried to figure out what they should do for a living, and all the while they kept selling these renovated trailers. A very slow lightbulb went off and they thought, *Well, maybe we are actually doing it?*

Anna said, "It was very surprising to us that people were buying trailers in the middle of the recession. We had people coming from all across the country to buy these trailers."

VIEW ONLINE

FLYTECAMP.COM

This 1959 Airstream Globester is extremely rare, produced through the California factory as a special order. This little beauty has been lovingly restored by Flyte Camp, and it resides at The Vintages trailer resort in Oregon. See page 151.

There is a certain generation of people who want to recapture the outdoor experiences of their youth, by exploring national parks and being outdoors. This resurgence of people with a love of the outdoors were the ultimate clientele of the newly formed Flyte Camp. Flyte Camp blossomed, and turned from a hobby into a business. Today, Anna and Justin have created one of the most successful trailer-renovation companies in the United States and are featured on the TV show *Flippin' RVs*.

Anna and Justin work predominantly with pre-1965 trailers, as the methods of the aircraft construction and the authenticity of the interior materials really appeal to them. For most trailers after 1965, or for Airstreams after 1969, the methods of construction changed to include lighter-weight paneling and fiberglass interiors. When redesigning trailers, Anna and Justin look to the era of the trailer to give them inspiration, and use materials that would have been employed at the time. They capture the authentic feeling of the era in the trailer with honest materials and textures that reflect the period. An Airstream is the one type of trailer that they feel they can add more of a modern touch to, mainly because the shape of the exterior and the aluminum interior panels lend themselves to almost any era or influence.

This beautiful example of Flyte Camp's 1957 Sovereign of the Road can be found at The Vintages trailer resort in Oregon. The exterior remains as they found it—but the interior has a stunning Scandinavian design that gave it a new-century feel. Anna says the "design really pops with it and gives people different ideas on what you can do!"

"WE BELIEVE IN 'GO WEST, YOUNG WOMAN!' GETTING OUT ON THE OPEN ROAD TO US HAS BEEN ONE OF THE MOST IMPORTANT WAYS WE'VE BUILT OUR BUSINESS, AND OUR LIVES. IT'S AMAZING WHAT YOU LEARN ABOUT LIFE AND YOURSELF WHEN YOU'RE OUT WANDERING ABOUT."

JUNK GYPSY

Junk Gypsy is an antique ("junk") business built on a wing and a prayer by three kindred spirits. Amie and Jolie Sikes are the face of Junk Gypsy, a family-run business started by the two sisters along with their mom, Janie, based out of Round Top, Texas. They embody the wandering spirit and the freedom of the open road, and combine it with the drive and passion to follow their hearts.

After college, Amie and Jolie tried out the real world and both fell into respectable jobs. But the draw of the creative wandering spirit called them home, and in 1998, Junk Gypsy was formed. With a fascination for all things junk and vintage, combined with a wanderlust spirit, they soon brought Airstreams into the mix. The Junk Gypsies' dear friend Miranda Lambert asked a favor: Would they design and build her an Airstream to take with her on tour? Of course they said yes, and embarked on their first Airstream redesign.

"Airstreams speak to us," Amie says. "It is an American-designed, American-made American dream. They embody the great American road trip, and each one has its own open-road story to tell. To us, the iconic Airstream became a symbol of a better way to get from here to there, literally and figuratively."

Since then the Junk Gypsies have renovated five Airstreams in total, including ones for Amie, Dierks Bentley, Green Day's Billie Joe Armstrong, and Miranda's mom, Bev Lambert. Although Amie and Jolie don't create Airstreams for the masses, their design process and true wandering spirit is a beautiful inspiration to those who are about to begin designing their own Airstreams.

VIEW ONLINE

GYPSYVILLE.COM

Amie says, "Everyone is better when they can live in a space, or roam a country in a space, that really speaks to them—and at the same time feels like an escape."

"We couldn't ever be decorators for a living because we get so immersed in it," Amie says. "When we did Billie Joe's, for instance, we watched every documentary that has ever been done on Green Day, listened to all of the albums over and over a million times—his wife sent us anything special she could that would resonate with him. We got inside his world, and then gave him our version of what that looks like to us, and what we felt like he would like. We want to know that the design of a personal Airstream means something to them, resonates with them. It's not just furniture, paint, and art on the walls. If there isn't a meaning behind the design, it doesn't mean anything for us. And that meaning is individualistic for every person."

Junk Gypsies share more of their design style and inspiration through their TV show *Junk Gypsies*, a beautiful store in Round Top, and a fantastic book out, *Junk Gypsy: Designing a Life at the Crossroads of Wonder & Wander*, featuring more of their design projects.

AMIE SIKES

"WHEN YOUR DAUGHTER IS TWO, THE WHOLE WORLD IS SPARKLES, FRINGE, AND EVERYTHING PINK. MY AIRSTREAM IS LIKE A LOVE STORY TO MY TWO-YEAR-OLD BABY GIRL."

Miranda Lambert's Airstream, the Junk Gypsies' first Airstream makeover.

Amie Sikes's Airstream, inspired by her daughter.

Dierks's Airstream

"Dierks's trailer has an authentic troubadour Nashville, American kind of look," Amie recalls. "He wanted it to be two things, a place where he could go camping with his wife and kids, but he also wanted it to be a place he could drink moonshine and write music with the boys in the band. So we thought to ourselves, okay, this has got to have a double duty. This has got to be a family place but has also got to be a really swanky hangout."

Billie Joe's Airstream

Amie describes Billie Joe's unique Airstream as "the ultimate surf shack with a bit of punk rocker." Amie recalls, "We love it because it was a little different than anything we had done before, so it challenged us. It was a twentieth wedding anniversary gift from his wife, a place that was to be all his own. So we wanted to create the bed as a nook, where he would be able to write music, cocoon, and escape."

Veteran Airstream DIYer Kristiana Spaulding's Bambi II, a rare beauty lovingly cared for.

DESIGNING YOUR OWN AIRSTREAM

DIY CREATION

MAKING AN AIRSTREAM YOUR OWN

Whether your Airstream is new off the factory floor, or a completely gutted shell stripped to its bare bones, you will need to decide how you make it your own. The wonderful thing about small spaces is that they really make you think about what is really important. People may buy a bigger TV or a bigger kitchen, just to fill the space of a house. Owning an Airstream forces you to be a conscientious consumer, makes you appreciate the little things, and helps you focus on what makes you truly happy.

Creating an Airstream of your own also brings a freedom—not just the freedom of the open road, but also the freedom to be yourself. Sometimes we feel pressured to present our homes with the latest "in" designs, or have financial constraints. Airstream allows the freedom to choose what you truly want. You can buy that top-quality countertop because you need only four feet of it to fit an Airstream, not the twenty-four feet that you would need to fit around your kitchen at home. You can buy that incredible, unique piece of furniture or light fixture because you need only one, not ten. Maybe you have always wanted an entire home decorated with a Hawaiian theme, or you want to paint the whole room blue from top to bottom. Somehow, Airstreams give us that freedom to say, Yes, I will decorate my entire Airstream in a cowboy theme, or paint it a hair-raising shade of red, just because I can and it makes me happy.

Renovation versus Restoration

More than 60 percent of all of the Airstreams ever made are still on the road today, and the demand for them has never been higher. Prices are rising, and the ability to find one in good condition is becoming more difficult with every passing year. Before you start looking, you should decide if are you looking to renovate or restore. Renovation means removing a substantial amount of the original features to build in your own design. Restoration is working to return the Airstream as closely as possible to its original condition. This can still mean upgrades and technological advances, along with sympathetic updates to the fabrics and soft furnishings, but when you walk into a restored Airstream, you will feel as though you have just have stepped back in time. It's important to know if you intend to renovate or restore before buying your Airstream, as it's a real shame when someone purchases a good-condition vintage Airstream, only to tear it to pieces and leave it as a gutted project. If your intention is to gut an Airstream, ideally look to buy one that has already been gutted or in which the interior hasn't fared too well for its age—it will also be cheaper.

DIY or Professional Help?

If you have the finances to cover it, getting a professional to be a part of the project is ideal. You can be involved in the design, but skip cleaning out the black water tank and pulling out the rodent-infested insulation. Professionals also have the skills to address issues that you may not consider until you are halfway through your project, such as how to make tiles stay on the walls of a trailer that, while rolling down the road, is in the equivalent of a 7.8 earthquake.

Even though designing and building your own Airstream can be half the fun of owning one, please be realistic about what you can take on. We get excited about all those beautiful pictures of stunning Airstreams and are swayed by the lifestyle that they can offer, so we can sometimes jump in headfirst without really thinking of what that means. So many people start out with the best intentions, but unfortunately the market is now flooded with half-finished and gutted Airstreams, because the project just got too big for them. When speaking to the many people I have met on my travels, the one thing that I hear again and again is to assess your own capabilities before jumping in. If you don't have mechanical know-how or lack experience in rebuilding, then this may not be for you.

Luckily, there is also a happy medium: allocate the funds to get help where you need it and do the work you have the skills for yourself. This will help the budget, and also help the project get finished.

FINDING A VINTAGE TRAILER

You've decided a vintage trailer is for you and you are jumping in hook, line, and sinker! If you're still deciding on length or year, check out the sections on Airstream design (page 29) and full-time Airstream living (page 107). Once you have this in mind, you can start investigating how to acquire one.

Airstream Classifieds and Craigslist are the most easily accessible and easiest to navigate. Airstream Classifieds is a great place to find unique and high-end renovated and restored Airstreams. If you want your budget to stretch a little further, you may have to spend some time on a treasure hunt. Craigslist is also a good place to start, but it does take a bit of time to search different areas. Also try Airstream Facebook groups and communities, one of these groups, Airstream Hunter, lists a variety of Airstreams for sale. If you live in America, one of the best places to start is actually your own neighborhood. Ask people you know—ask on social media, post pictures of what you are looking for, and keep a lookout for unloved Airstreams in someone's yard.

So you think you have found one, the price sounds good, and you have fallen in love with it just from the pictures. No one can talk you out of it now! But just for a minute put your heart back in your chest and consider the practicalities.

There is a little saying in the vintage trailer community: "There are only two kinds of trailers, those that leak and those that are gonna leak." Find out how bad the leaks are. Has your trailer been left out in the weather to continue leaking, or has it been stored in a dry place where the weather hasn't taken its toll?

Look at the furniture and flooring, and around the windows, doors, vents, A/C, and any other places where there is an opening to the exterior. Check every corner of the floor, especially near the bathroom, and under beds and storage units—is the floor soft? Take a moisture gauge with you if the owner will allow you to use it; it could tell you a lot. If there is light damage, maybe you can seal the leak and replace the damaged fittings. But if it's major, you may need to replace a rusted-out chassis and a rotted floor. One thing that should set off alarm bells is "new flooring," especially if it's just a top-level vinyl floor cover. Ask if you can pull it back to see the real floor underneath. Leak damages are going to be a major cost when renovating a trailer, so be serious about taking time to look for water damage. If you can get to or see the chassis, make sure you investigate that for rust and damage too. But given there will more than likely be a belly pan and a floor in your way, this may be rather difficult.

Inspect the shell to see if there are dents, holes, or any other kind of damage. Dents can be easy to pop out on some trailers, but can mean panel replacement on others. Take some photos to a professional and ask for advice. Panel replacement in new or vintage trailers can be an expensive task, so it's something to consider when adding up the budget.

When shopping for an Airstream, don't be tempted to be cheap. It will be worth it in the long run to spend a bit more to buy a trailer in good working order rather than having to fund the reinstallation of plumbing and wiring or a new floor and chassis later down the road.

Kristiana Spaulding finds her dream trailer, an Airstream Argosy, through a fortunate conversation only a few miles away from her home.

 **TOP 10** **QUESTIONS TO ASK WHEN BUYING A TRAILER**

1

Where has it been stored? Has it become home to any critters?

2

How long have you owned it, and what do you know about its history?

3

Do all of the systems work—A/C, electricity, gas, plumbing?

4

Is there any floor rot?

5

Are there any leaks?

6

Is there any rust on the chassis?

7

When was the last time the trailer was used?

8

Are there any issues with the tires or axles?

9

What condition is the shell in? Are there any dents or signs of damage?

10

What condition are the interior furnishings in?

THE FIRST DIY STEPS

Safety and Trailer First Aid

When picking up your trailer, pay particular attention to the axles and chassis. Taking a few things with you when you head out to pick up your trailer will help you have a safe ride home. Duct tape seems to be everyone's go-to item to secure anything that may become a hazard. Kristiana Spaulding, veteran Airstream DIYer, also notes when she picks up a trailer for the first time, she never leaves home without a flashlight, painter's tape (as duct tape can sometimes leave a mark), temporary tow lights, zip ties, and a portable air compressor for flat tires. If you're going more than a few miles back home, take the Airstream to a mechanic to ensure the wheels, tires, and axles are safe for the journey.

Once home, apply some trailer first aid as soon as possible. Check the exterior for any broken seals between panels and vents in the exterior, windows and doors, broken windows or latches, etc., and seal them up. You want to weatherproof your trailer as fast as possible. That may mean getting out the sealant, duct-taping over holes in the shell, or taping down a window to keep it temporarily closed. Ideally you want to be working on your trailer in good weather, or have a garage or storage space to protect your Airstream from the elements.

Photos, Lots of Them!

Grab your camera and take lots—*I mean lots*—of photos. Not only do they give you those all-important before and after photos, but they also give you a record of any problem spots that you may clean away or paint over.

Photo from the day Kristiana acquired her new Argosy.

Cleaning and Testing

This is a tad self-explanatory, but be prepared to clean years of grime and dirt and, if you are extra lucky, the remains of small animals that once made your Airstream their home. This part really wasn't at the top of your list when you were dreaming of creating your own Airstream, but it's necessary.

Cleaning every corner of your Airstream allows you to really get to know the new addition to your family. Keep a running list of areas that need a bit of love and attention, whether it's a window catch or a hinge that needs fixing, or something that no amount of cleaning will bring back to life and you will need to replace. Keep an eye out for signs of leaks, and note them on a diagram. And while the plumbing system, including the black water tank, could be the most unpleasant thing in your Airstream, it needs to be dealt with and flushed out.

As the list grows and the days of cleaning add up, the job can feel discouraging, so as Kristiana says, "Mix it up with some of the fun things about renovating an Airstream." While you're cleaning, display some fabric swatches or inspiration boards. Take some time out and just be in your trailer. You may want to focus on cleaning the dinette first so you have somewhere to sit.

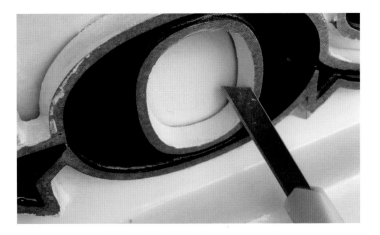

Assessing

Once you have your to-do list to get your trailer in tip-top shape, you need to start breaking it down: deciphering costs, learning how to fix things, finding where to get replacement parts, and deciding who is going to tackle each task.

Throughout your cleaning process, you have more than likely come across things that are mysterious to you. As previously mentioned, there really aren't great records of all models and features, but fortunately you have just entered into a very passionate and supportive community of people who are more than happy to help and share their knowledge.

Air Forums is a great place to start. It can be a little hard to navigate and find exactly what you need, but if you can't find it, feel free to start a thread and ask members your questions—they more than likely have years of experience tracking down the very same answers you are searching for. There are many members who have renovated and restored trailers and posted online tutorials, or tips and tricks to make a restorer's life easier.

When you're looking for replacement parts and design inspiration, a great place to start is Vintage Trailer Supply, an online store. They provide a range of era-appropriate features and replica replacement parts such as light casings and fittings, along with how-to guides, like an in-depth guide on how to polish your Airstream to a mirror shine.

If you are looking for something a bit different, you may also want to try the marine-grade fixtures and fittings used in the building of luxury yachts. These are also designed for small spaces, and they offer a range of unique design styles that may not be available in trailer catalogs.

Once you have exhausted all your online resources, it's a good idea to check in with a professional. Get him or her to assess all your structural elements and systems. If you are going to spend any time out on the open road, making sure you are safe is priority number one.

GETTING CREATIVE

Kristiana Spaulding

Kristiana Spaulding is a name that is well-known in the Airstream industry. With an intense love for silver for as long as she can remember, Kristiana is a silver-jewelry maker with an undeniable infatuation with Airstreams. Combining her intuitive eye for aesthetics and her dedication to authentic design, Kristiana has spent more than ten years bringing Airstream trailers back to life. She is not afraid to get her hands dirty, and works hard to make sure that every inch of her trailer is how she envisaged it.

Kristiana restores vintage Airstreams, of which she currently has eight. She uses them for her own outdoor adventures, and provides them as rentals for weddings and special occasions as well. They also have been featured in several books, magazines, television shows, and advertisements. Kristiana was integral to the beginnings of Airstream 2 Go, owned by previous Airstream CEO and President Dicky Riegel, and also assisted in the supply of Airstreams for Zappos CEO Tony Hsieh, for his Las Vegas Airstream trailer park. She is well and truly, as they say in the Airstream community, "infected with silver."

VIEW ONLINE

SILVERTRAILER.COM

Spend Time in Your Trailer

One of Kristiana's tips for the DIY process is to spend time in your trailer before you start making big decisions about how you are going to make it your own. Have your morning coffee in your Airstream as it sits in your driveway, and imagine how you could use the spaces and how it's going to feel spending long periods of time in it. Take the trailer out for a weekend, test it out, and figure out what is working, what needs fixing, and what needs changing.

Inspiration Boards

You have the practicalities sorted, and hopefully a good idea of how you want the space to feel and how you want it to be used. Now you want to find the look for your Airstream interior: what fabrics you are going to use and what features you are going to need.

Kristiana starts by finding one or two points of inspiration: a person, a place, an object, or even a memory. Take photos of this inspiration, and pin them up alongside the photos of your Airstream in its "before" condition, as the starting point of your inspiration board. This could be a physical pin board, or a binder full of thoughts and ideas, or it could be digital, such as a designated Pinterest board or a store wish list. Kristiana likes the physical, tangible boards but finds the digital side also very helpful.

Find images, fabric swatches, natural materials, items, and textures to add to your inspiration board. Search magazines and go online to find images that fit your vision. You may replace images throughout the process as you discover new looks, but keep the superseded images in a folder as you never know what you may come back to.

Kristiana's inspiration boards for her newly acquired Argosy.

ARGOSY
BY KRISTIANA

Trailers just seem to find their way to Kristiana, and her latest addition was no different. When an Argosy owner who lived three miles down the road was looking for a jeweler, she tracked down Kristiana. She started conversing with Kristiana via email, but as soon as she saw her email signature she put two and two together and replied "I have an Argosy for sale, are you interested?" An Argosy was the last Airstream on Kristiana's list of dream trailers that she wanted to acquire, and so, long story short, Kristiana soon had a 1972 Argosy trailer parked in her driveway.

Not long after her new purchase, she was off on a dream trip to Africa, heading out on safari and staying at one of the most well-known Airstream hotels in the Southern Hemisphere. The textures of the African landscape, colors of the traditional arts, and textiles of the safari tents all inspired the creation of Kristiana's Argosy interior design.

She pinned up souvenirs and photos of her recent travels through Africa, Mexico, and California next to photos of her newly acquired Argosy. Kristiana also incorporated into the design the memory of a dear friend who had passed away. Her middle name was Acacia, which was the name Kristiana gave her Argosy. Acacia is also a beautiful and tough tree found on the plains of Africa. Kristiana's inspiration board grew, adding found items, photographs, and printed materials.

Through the process of bringing the Argosy back to life with its new African persona, the dilapidated carpet was replaced, the bathroom was restored to its original fixtures, every corner was cleaned and steam-cleaned, broken parts were replaced, and the inspiration board was incorporated from the design of the lamps to the details on the accessories. Even a photograph Kristiana had taken in Tanzania was integrated directly into the design, becoming a shower curtain and printed on fabric for pillows. The result is an authentic original Argosy trailer, with a lifeblood all its own.

FINDING YOUR FLOOR PLAN

If you are restoring a trailer you will have a floor plan to work with, but if you are renovating you may have a lot more options on how you want to organize your space.

There are going to be many things that influence your floor layout, but the most important thing to consider is how you intend to use your Airstream. Is it going to be a guesthouse in the back of the yard or a vacation house you visit once a year that stays in one location? Is it a holiday house on wheels or a full-time abode? Your needs are going to be different depending on the scenario.

There are some constraints to consider while designing your floor plan. First and foremost is the way in which Airstream trailers are round at the edges, reducing head height around the periphery. Walkways need to be as central as possible, providing space to maneuver without banging your head. You also have the wheel wells, and no matter how awkward you think they are, you definitely can't go moving those. Generally, Airstreams have bathrooms, storage cabinets, or beds over wheel wells to try and make the best of the remaining space around them.

When designing your layout, make sure every space has a use—if not two or three uses. It may be a good idea to make a plan and diagram how you may use each space to determine if it needs any reconfiguration for its intended use.

When you start to get into the technical challenges of restoration, including new wiring, plumbing, removal of interior panels, or even full shell-off restorations (removing of the shell from the flooring and chassis), a good place to start would be to read through Air Forums and listen to *VAP* (*Vintage Airstream Podcast*). Many experienced restorers are a part of the Air Forums community, and Colin Hyde, a well-known vintage trailer restorer, features on *VAP*.

Drawing Out Your Plans

Why not take a page from Wally's book? Wally had a unique method for designing interiors. He would lay huge rolls of butcher paper out on the floor and begin to draw the trailer and its floor plan, life-size. This gives you a really good idea about how spaces will work, and gives you a feeling for the size of your trailer—but don't forget you have a curved shell above your head while walking around your butcher-paper Airstream layout!

the PLAN

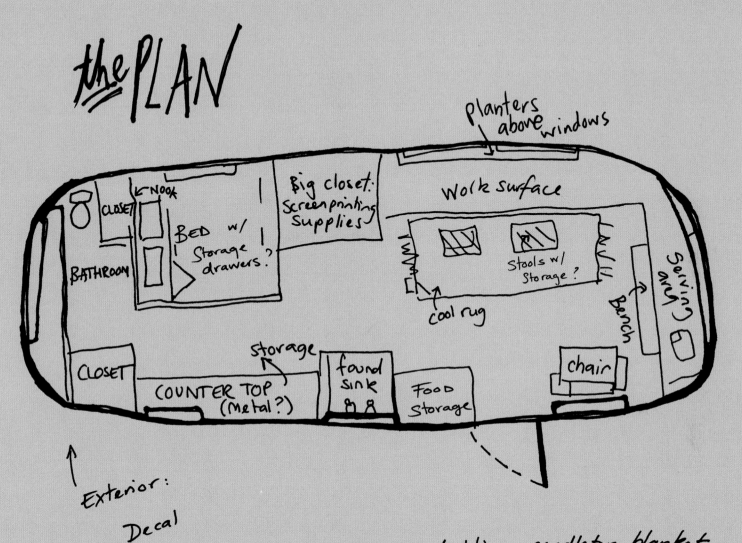

planters above windows

Work surface

CLOSET · NOOK

Big closet:
Screenprinting
Supplies

BED w/
Storage
drawers ?

BATHROOM

Stools w/
Storage ?

cool rug

Bench

Serving area

CLOSET

storage

found
sink

chair

COUNTER TOP
(Metal ?)

Food
Storage

Exterior:

Decal

Find: Cool rug, reclaimed redwood, lighting, pendleton blanket,
found furniture? skulls, old flag... sink w/ unique faucet,
Planters? metal and wood

Considerations for Full-time Living

Airstream floor plans may be slightly different if you are full-timing versus using the trailer as a holiday home or guesthouse. You may like to think about or, even better, test out some of the following considerations.

Bathroom Configuration

Some Airstreams feature a shower separate from the toilet/sink, each positioned on opposite sides of the hallway. Others feature a complete bathroom on the side, or at the rear. There are pluses and minuses to all configurations. A separate shower helps with the containment of condensation, and also allows for someone else to be using the toilet or sink while you are taking your shower. On the other hand, stepping out from the shower straight into the hallway can be a bit awkward, especially when it comes to privacy.

Kitchen Amenities and Appliances

RV freezers are not the most reliable. While RV fridges do tend to keep cold, freezers fluctuate—so storage of frozen meats or foods on a long-term basis is not wise. Consider your fridge size in comparison with how many family members are on board, as well as how long you may need to store food. If you intend to boondock on a regular basis, you will need to stock up, but if you are passing through towns and staying in RV parks, you will be able to do more regular shopping. When considering your cupboard configuration, allow for a good-sized pantry as a lot of your cooking may revolve around food that can be easily stored long-term.

Dedication of Personal Space

If you are a couple, most spaces will function as they were generally designed and intended. But if you are living with a family, consider dividing up the Airstream to make all family members feel as if they have their own personal space, no matter how small. It is important for both children and adults to feel at home.

Winter Heating and Ventilation

While many Airstreams have good heaters installed to keep you warm in the winter, the cold weather can come with another practical issue. Keeping your windows and doors closed to keep warm during the cold weather can make it very difficult to remove excess condensation caused by heaters, cooking, breathing, and showering. During the summer months, you will be living with your doors, windows, and ventilation hatches open, but as the winter months roll around, the last thing you want to do is let the freezing cold air in. Installing a good ventilation system is key if you intend to live there full time in the winter: including hoods over your exterior vents so even when it's raining you can still let the condensation out.

Engineering and Weight Distribution

Airstreams are known for their light weight and their majestic handling—this is an engineering marvel—so be careful not to mess with perfection. Find a trailer with a layout that is close to what you want, this will save you a lot of hassle down the track trying to move a bathroom, kitchen, or heavy appliances with all their embedded systems—and still have a trailer that will pull safely.

Changing a floor plan is not impossible but it can be a challenging engineering feat. Many professional designers have a lot of experience and tools at their disposal to consider the impact of moving items from their original positions, and they almost always rebuild or at least restructure the entire chassis to not only fit the changing weights of the floor layout but also avoid the liabilities of an old, structurally unsound chassis.

Storage

Think about storage like playing a game of *Tetris*: If you put that thing there, how is it going to affect the other things around it? Think about the items you use the most and make these the most easily accessible.

Also think about the items you are buying in the first place: Can they stack inside each other? Do you really need that massive frying pan? How many glasses do you really need? You will have friends over, but think a little about how many and how often.

THE HARD WORK . . .

Owning an Airstream is going to be a fun, educational, satisfying, and sometimes frustrating experience. You are definitely going to have to put in the hard work to create your new dream home on wheels, but remember, you are part of the Airstream community now. Reach out to them online or at a local rally whenever you need support. They are a great community and are as excited about your journey as they are about their own Airstream journey.

As you take your Airstream on its first journey with your family, you will have entered a new way of living, a new way to see life and experience all it has to offer. You have now officially entered the Airstream way of life!

"THERE IS SO MUCH BEAUTY IN LIVING SIMPLY."

THE LOCAL BRANCH

Mackenzie and Blaine are an exceptionally creative couple whose handcrafted artisanal goods business, combined with wanderlust, led them to the Airstream way of life. In 2012, they set out to find and create their new home. They had limited funds, but a Kickstarter project gave them the funds to purchase their $3,000 1978 32' Sovereign Land Yacht.

They found their Airstream looking very forlorn, with broken windows, flat tires, graffiti, and even some unidentifiable green slime on the interior walls. But despite all this, the body and frame were in good shape—there was no rust or rotting. Having never towed before, they bought their first hitch from Walmart and tentatively towed their new Airstream back to San Francisco.

Timing was tight, as they had given notice on their apartment and needed to move into their new Airstream home as soon as possible. The Airstream sat on a residential street in San Francisco when the renovation work began. Mackenzie recalls, "Ripping out the damaged interior was a crazy two-day journey, dealing with some of the most disgusting substances on earth." They gutted most of the dilapidated interior, cleaned every surface and fixture, and added a fresh coat of paint. The next step was to take their new home to a professional to check the axles, tires, and chassis, along with all the systems. They were taking to the road full time, and needed to make sure that everything was safe, reliable, and in good working order.

The interior design started with a floor plan sketch, featured on page 95, and was inspired by the different materials and items they collected from local salvage yards. They came across reclaimed redwood, which not only was a great material to feature in their Airstream, but also was a very practical choice for their cupboard lining. It was very old and dry, and split very thinly, making it extremely light and a wonderful texture to contrast against the aluminum. Most of the interior items were sourced from salvage yards and often repurposed or combined with other items to have a dual purpose.

One of their biggest decisions regarding the floor plan was to remove the shower to create additional storage. As they were both living and working out of their Airstream, they needed to consider every space and how it could work for them. They decided that the inconvenience of showering in campgrounds and RV parks was worth the additional storage space.

They both had experience in set design and builds, as well as designing interior spaces, so taking on a challenge of renovating an Airstream wasn't too daunting for the couple. Using the knowledge they had and the resources and information available online, they built their new home. They fixed the plumbing, the interior wall panels, the flooring, and installed the space dividers and the new large workbench, and also polished the exterior of the trailer.

Mackenzie and Blaine took their business, the Local Branch, out on the open road. They settled into their home and workshop space, happy with the choices they had made through their design process. They had created a work space up front and a comfortable living space in the rear. A lot of the little interior design touches came from their first few months of travel on the road, stopping at antiques stores and collecting memories along the way.

KATIE AND ROB

Katie and Rob are two of the most lovely, genuine, caring people I've ever met. Their door is always open, and walking into their 1986 Excella Airstream feels like being welcomed home. This is one of the five Airstreams they own, but this one is extra special. This thirty-two-foot beauty was originally designed to sleep four comfortably, six if needed—but Katie and Rob have a family of nine, twelve if you count the grandparents. That is seven children! Having a family this large might stop the average family from taking a holiday, but Rob and Katie found a way to take their children and their parents on an Airstream journey of a lifetime.

Katie's father was an architect, so she picked up a thing or two from him, and has an excellent eye for design. Rob is a meticulous craftsman, making sure everything he builds is thoughtfully created and beautifully executed. Together they set about making their Airstream to fit the whole family. Their number one priority was to make sure that everybody had their own little space, no matter how small, as long as it was theirs. The back bedroom became the

kids' space, with four bunks and a foldout bed. This space can also be used by the children to play board games, read books, or just have some time to relax. Along the hallway the storage cupboards were removed to feature two more bunks across from the bathroom. Under all these bunks are sliding cabinets where the kids can keep their personal belongings. The bathroom stayed in its original location, beautifully restored. Katie and Rob removed the gaucho (sofa bed), and in its place put a double bed for them to sleep, with a massive storage area underneath, including the all-important wine rack. Along the side wall where the dinette had been, Rob and Katie devised a long couch that converts into a single and double bed, creating an Airstream that sleeps twelve.

Living in a trailer with this many people could end up making you feel like you are living on top of one another. However, thanks to a few clever choices made in the design and also some thoughtful choices in the way they live, staying in this Airstream makes everyone a happy camper.

Storage is always high on the priority list for any Airstreamer, as is having a place to sit down (especially with twelve people). Rob and Katie combined the two, creating great little storage containers that double as seating. One of the most unique things they have designed is a foldout dining table with stools that seats twelve comfortably. Rob and Katie also decided to install a dishwasher in their Airstream. This is probably what you would consider a luxury in camping, but the time it saves when washing dishes for a family of nine (and sometimes twelve) was worth the extra cost. Additionally, they color-coded everything—cups, dishes, etc.—so everyone has their own designated dishes so they don't have to constantly reach for a new glass or plate, leading to never-ending dirty dishes.

"MOM, WHAT DO YOU WANT TO LIVE IN
A TRAILER FOR???"

THREE POINTS RANCH

Three Points Ranch is an exceptionally special place. Sitting an hour out of Austin, Texas, the ranch is filled with family history, love, memories, and a warm energy that hits you the moment you head down the driveway. Sally Thompson has been a fan of vintage Airstreams for a very long time, long before they became popular or seen as a fashionable accessory. Much to the displeasure of her young children at the time, she bought her first Airstream to use as a permanent home in 1995.

Sally's grandparents' ranch was divided up among the grandchildren, so she had inherited some land. She didn't have enough money to build anything at the time, so she chose to buy an Airstream instead, living happily on her land for several years. She loved her Airstream so much that she began collecting them. She now has nine, dating from the '50s to the '70s. Sally loves design and uses each Airstream as a place to decorate and redecorate a very special and personal space.

With her ranch and her collection of Airstreams, Sally formed the Three Point Ranch Wedding Venue in 2008. Each of her Airstreams had a purpose during each wedding and ceremony. There was the wedding's central office, the bride's trailer, the groom's trailer, and the extra special trailer sitting at the entrance to the ceremony, where the bride waited to take her walk down the aisle. Each interior was designed with its use in mind, and Sally's creativity and admiration for the silver bullets brings together a unique style all unto itself. Simple interiors allow for detailed and thoughtful furnishings.

Recently, the Three Point Ranch transitioned into an exceptional glamping (glamorous camping) experience. Whether you wish to hold a yoga retreat or a gathering of friends and family, this unique ranch in the Texas landscape is definitely a once-in-a-lifetime experience that should not be missed.

The son of children's book writers Mark and Rowan Sommerset, Linden, wakes up daily to the Airstream life.

FULL-TIME AIRSTREAM LIVING

BUYING AN AIRSTREAM

When buying your Airstream, you have a lot of things to consider, both practical and emotional.

If you are using it for full-time travel versus a guesthouse in the backyard, you will need to consider the Airstream's durability on the road. But if it is going to just sit and be a guesthouse or office or even a bar in your backyard, you won't need to focus so much on the durability and condition of the chassis, axles, and wheels.

When it comes to aesthetic and personality, some people are just vintage people, and others would only ever want new. So you need to figure out what era really appeals to you and see if it fits into your budget. Check out the chapter on Airstream design (page 29) to get an understanding of how Airstream design has changed over the years.

When choosing a size, think about where you may want to go. If you want to spend time in national parks, especially older parks, size can definitely be a factor. The older sites weren't built for thirty-four-foot trailers (and some weren't built for trailers at all). Road access may be difficult, and if you are not good at backing a trailer, you will need to look for pull-through sites. Some parks have a length limit on the trailers allowed in the park, either because the sites themselves can't accommodate longer trailers or there just isn't any access. If you stick to twenty-five feet and smaller there shouldn't be many places you can't go, but then again this does reduce your living space. Cost is also going to factor into size choice, in regard to not only purchase prices but also ongoing maintenance. You'll need to think about how many people you'll be accommodating: Do they want a permanent bed, or will a foldout suffice? Don't forget to include space consideration for guests.

Exporting an Airstream

Exporting an Airstream, new or used, outside the United States is going to be costly. You will of course have transportation costs, but don't forget duty and taxes. Also in some countries, like Australia, it is a requirement to have the door moved to the other side of the trailer, which is fine if it's new—there are Australian-designed Airstreams available—but if they are vintage it's a big cost and also a big design change to the original trailer to move a door. To import an Airstream into any country you are looking at an extra cost of at least $12,000 to $15,000, but that's very dependent on the country and its specific rules. Best to touch base with someone who has been there and done that to get a more accurate assessment.

TOP 10 QUESTIONS TO ASK WHEN BUYING AN AIRSTREAM

1

Traveling: Where are you going to go in your Airstream? Boondocking, national parks, or RV parks? All of the above?

2

Sleeping configurations: How many people will it need to sleep? And is it important to have a permanent bed, or are you happy to set it up each night?

3

Transporting equipment: Do you have any large items (kayaks, bikes, skis, etc.) that you need to transport?

4

Entertaining: Do you entertain often? Do you need to consider space for guests?

5

Style: What era shell and/or interior suits your personal style?

6

Size: How long do you need your Airstream to be? The longer it is, the more room you have, yes, but also a greater upfront cost, higher upkeep expenses, and reduced maneuverability.

7

Bathroom: Do you want the bathroom to be in the center or the tail? If it's in the center, do you want the shower separate from the toilet and sink? Can you live with a wet bath (the toilet, shower, and sink are all in a shower-sized room)?

8

Furniture: Are you planning to work out of your trailer? Is it important to have a dinette? Or just a couch/gaucho?

9

Towing: What can your tow vehicle actually tow? Are you going to have to buy a new vehicle?

10

Cost: How much do you have to spend?

YOUR AIRSTREAM BUDGET

If you're looking to get the best value for your dollar, Airstreams from the 1980s into the early '90s are likely your best bet. One in good condition will currently go for around $15,000 to $20,000, and the quality of the workmanship is top-class. If an '80s trailer has been well taken care of, it will have stood the test of time and you will have to do little to bring it up to your needs and style. If you are looking for a smaller trailer, though, they are very hard to come by, as bigger was definitely better in the '80s. Popular sizes ranged from twenty-seven to thirty-four feet.

Any Airstream made before 1980 will require time and money to bring it up to scratch. That's not to say that you can't buy them in great condition, with the hard work already done for you, but it will cost you. At prices over $15,000 for a trailer in okay original condition, and over $40,000 for a DIY renovated or restored one, you are creeping up toward the price of a new Airstream. The plus side of buying vintage, though, is that you can spend less upfront if you are willing to do the restoration work yourself. This is what makes vintage a practical financial choice for some, though it still requires appropriate skills and dedication.

Airstream's top-of-the-market 2016 Land Yacht is a stunning collaboration between Airstream and Mauro Micheli, renowned yacht designer for Riva.

New Airstreams start around the $45,000 mark, but if you purchase one that's only a few years old, the price can come down to around $30,000 for a Bambi Sport. The practicalities of owning a newer Airstream are also a big bonus: not only are all your appliances and fittings new, but so are all of your systems. Your plumbing, electricity, axles, awnings, and leveling jacks will all work perfectly, and knowing that your trailer is tightly sealed and your components don't have any wear and tear definitely gives you peace of mind.

If you are looking for something top-of-the-line, the Land Yacht has an exquisite interior designed by Italian yacht designer Mauro Micheli, and features all the latest technology available in the industry, matched with a high-end design. This twenty-eight-foot beauty starts from just under $147,000. If you're considering these prices, another option is to hire a professional to create your own customized Airstream. The professional designers, like some featured earlier in this book, can take a vintage Airstream and refurbish it with modern interiors. Prices for these generally start at around $100,000, but can get up to $200,000, depending on the specs and materials used. A high-end professionally designed vintage trailer will generally cost more than buying a brand-new Airstream.

Whatever your budget, remember to allocate the cost of a tow vehicle. If you already have a vehicle that can pull a smaller Airstream, that may become a part of your decision-making process.

This stunning high-end renovation by ARC Airstreams, called the English Country Retreat, features not only quality furnishings and fittings but also leadlight windows and a fully functional fireplace.

TOW VEHICLE

It's important to understand how towing works before buying a trailer or tow vehicle.

Ideally you want to decide on your trailer, and then get a vehicle to match. This won't restrict your selection of the right Airstream for you, and will also allow you to choose a sufficient tow vehicle. If you go the other way around, be very clear about what your vehicle's tow rating is, and do not push a vehicle to its maximum. A tow vehicle may technically be able to pull an extreme load, but you also have to think about towing up a steep incline, stopping when headed downhill, and driving in bad weather or on uneven roads. The best tip is to make sure your vehicle's tow capability is well over what's required for your trailer.

Understanding the terminology and mathematics of towing is a bit of a complicated business, so make sure you talk to professionals about towing your chosen trailer in combination with your tow vehicle.

Antisway stabilizer bars and load-distributing hitches make your trailer more secure to tow. Antisway bars act like shock absorbers to reduce the possibly of sway leading to fishtailing, whereas a load-distributing hitch aims to distribute the trailer weight more evenly throughout your trailer and tow vehicle. Your best purchase is a hitch that incorporates both antisway and load-distribution measures.

One of the biggest fears for people starting out is backing up a trailer. This great little diagram from an '80s Airstream trailer manual breaks it down. Best tip, go slow.

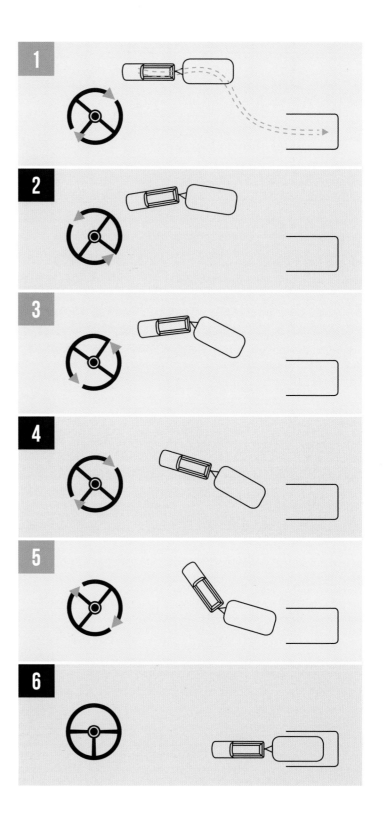

Airstream 2 Go's Airstream trailer and vehicle. Check out page 149 to see how you can go about renting this rig for your own Airstream adventure!

FINANCES

Setup Cost

After the cost of your Airstream and tow vehicle, your additional setup costs may include a generator, solar panel installation, a tow kit, wheel chocks, a tool kit, etc.

You will also need to consider whether you need new items, such as size-efficient kitchenware, storage boxes, containers, hooks, and other organization systems. You may also like to rent a storage unit for the things you already have that won't fit in your trailer (if you want to keep them!).

Day-to-day Costs

Day-to-day personal and food costs may not vary much from your lifestyle today, but your upkeep costs will be dramatically reduced. You can choose to live quite cheaply or very comfortably. I have met a few people who get by on $15,000 a year, but the majority of full-timers live comfortably on about $25,000 a year (plus any trailer or vehicle repayments).

There are basic elements that make up the cost of living full time in an RV:

Repayments on your Airstream and/or tow vehicle.

Site to park your Airstream.

Gas for your vehicle.

Maintenance of your vehicle and Airstream—e.g., tires, road taxes, services, etc.—as well as fixing anything that goes wrong.

Power (if not included in your site costs), generator fuel, or solar upkeep.

Cell phones and Wi-Fi.

PO box and mail redirecting.

Food. (This is one thing that does tend to go up, not down, mainly because you don't know where to get the best supermarket deals in each new town, and prices vary depending on your location. Also you're likely to eat out more than usual—it's easier, and it's also an opportunity to be social.)

Personal needs such as clothing, toiletries, and medical supplies.

RV and vehicle insurance.

Making an Income on the Road

The internet has definitely opened doors for a lot of people who are on the road full time. Web developers, programmers, graphic designers, writers, editors, and photographers, to name a few, all have a pretty straightforward time taking their job on the road. Small businesses that have an online store or presence—promoting their business in the cities and towns they visit—make the most of the opportunities that this lifestyle offers. Others incorporate living on the road into their way of making money, writing about it, organizing events for the community, or sharing their experiences and knowledge with others to help them become full-time travelers too.

Workamper.com offers seasonal or short-term jobs so that you can work in one place to earn money or work in lieu of paying for a site and utilities. You can also look for options through other short-term working programs such as WWOOF (World Wide Opportunities on Organic Farms).

Mackenzie and Blaine created the Local Branch, a company selling well-crafted artisanal goods in their online store and throughout the United States in the towns, festivals, and markets they visit in their Airstream trailer. Check out their site at www.thelocalbranch.co.

VIEW ONLINE

WWOOFUSA.ORG & WORKAMPER.COM

STAYING CONNECTED

WHERE TO PARK YOUR AIRSTREAM

Today, most countries have reliable cell phone and Internet access. Costs, as well as speed and reliability, vary from country to country, but you can generally make sure you have sufficient connection to the outside world. The majority of full-timers use their cell phone Internet plan as their online connection while traveling, although if you are working from home, you can chew through your plan's allowance pretty quickly. In the United States, full-timers who work from home spend between $200 to $350 per month on Internet charges. If you are freedom camping/boondocking, you may have trouble finding a strong signal, but investing in a signal booster will help.

Receiving mail is becoming less and less of an issue for those traveling full time. Set up a PO box and then redirect mail sent there to a local post office or RV park (check with them first) that you intend to cross paths with in your travels. You can also get large items sent straight to a specific post office or RV park.

You have a lot of options when it comes to parking your Airstream, but it all really depends on what kind of Airstream life you want to live.

RV parks offer a range of amenities and modern conveniences. Because of this, they usually cost more per night than other options. Budgeting around $35 per night would be a good starting point, but some parks in high-demand and popular areas can be more than $60 per night. Some RV parks in the United States also offer long-term sites, with monthly rates of about $450 to $600 plus power, depending on the location and the amenities available.

National parks offer the ability to get outdoors into nature, but still provide some amenities. You also have the comfort of others around, but still have a bit of space so it doesn't just feel like a parking lot (though some of the more popular parks can still feel this way, especially during peak season). Depending on the location and the popularity of the park, prices can vary dramatically but average around $15 to $20 per night.

Boondocking, or freedom camping, is camping without amenities, and relying on what you bring with you to cook, drink, shower, and source power. You can really get away from it all, be in the middle of nowhere, and enjoy the world around you. And it's free!

Campendium, an Airstream couple who have set up a great website for helping others find a place to stay with their Airstream, are setting up for their own boondocking adventure.

DAILY CHORES

Cooking in an Airstream is a little different than at home. The kitchen is smaller, so it tends to get messy pretty quickly, and the smells of cooking end up permeating every corner of your trailer. It may not be a great idea to cook a strong curry in your Airstream every night! Many full-timers use a combination of fresh vegetables and fruits along with dried or tinned goods, avoiding the use of the freezer when possible. Fresh salads and lightly cooked meals are ideal for the Airstream kitchen, but that's not to say that you can't cook a hearty beef casserole in your convection oven! Your other option is an outdoor kitchen—you can cook almost anything on a portable grill, even your Sunday roast. Dutch ovens are a unique way of cooking at a campsite. By heating up the oven with hot coals, you can make breakfast, desserts, and full meals.

Airstreams don't usually have a washing machine installed, so your laundry routine will need a bit of planning. RV parks have great facilities, and even if you boondock most of the time, staying in an RV park once in a while might be your opportunity to get your laundry done. Your other options include launderettes or small, hand-powered washers.

Emptying your tanks, especially your black water tank, can be quite the experience. But once you get used to the process, it all becomes part of everyday life.

Matt Hackney is a Dutch oven aficionado. Whether he's at Alumapalooza at the Airstream factory, or at the recent WBCCI rally, Matt can be found teaching everyone how versatile and easy Dutch oven cooking can be.

POWER (SOLAR, GENERATOR, OR HOOKUPS)

You are going to need power, and though your new Airstream will be set up for places with hookups, when you go off the beaten path even a little, you're going to need another power source. Even though it's a bit costly to set up, solar power can be cheaper in the long run, and won't spoil the peace and quiet of your site. The panels do require sunlight, so if you intend to stay somewhere without reliable sunshine hours, you will need a backup generator. Choosing a quiet and efficient generator will not only give you the best use of fuel, but also keep your neighbors happy. Stinky, loud generators do not make happy neighbors. You can get solar kits for about $600, and a fully installed system can be up to $2,800, although that price is reducing all the time as better technology is introduced. Speak with a professional to find out what your lifestyle will require. Generators are getting cheaper, and you can get them secondhand, but be prepared to spend about $700 on a decent one.

Campendium, boondocking with their Airstream buddies, utilizing their fantastic solar setup that supplies them with all the power they need.

PLANNING YOUR JOURNEY

So you are all sorted, have your Airstream, and are ready to hit the road. But where to?

Leigh, an Airstream full-timer, cofounder of Campendium, and avid journey planner, suggests first and foremost to follow the weather. Airstreams are equipped with great A/C systems and good heaters, but it's best to stick to a comfortable temperature and not rely on hookups or power usage. Even the best A/C can only bring your temperature down about ten to fifteen degrees, so sitting in the middle of Death Valley in the height of summer is going to get uncomfortable pretty quickly. Secondly, Leigh suggests, if you intend on heading anywhere popular, getting your reservations there confirmed first and then scheduling your trip around that. Places in the Florida Keys, Yosemite, and southern Utah sell out within minutes of becoming available, even when reservations open up eleven months in advance. Because of work commitments and the places they want to visit (and because she just loves planning!), Leigh likes to plan their journey over a year in advance. Other Airstreamers just like to wing it, although this only really works if you are a full-time boondocker or just happy to go with the flow when your first choice (or even your second) isn't available.

Teresa and Glenn Taylor's collection of postcards pinned to the inside of their stunningly restored 1968 International Airstream.

CAMPENDIUM

When you are looking for the ideal place to park your Airstream, the Campendium website is the perfect place to start your journey. Two full-time Airstreamers, Leigh and Brian, created the site to assist all those who travel in a trailer to find their home for the night. They offer thousands of listings of campsites throughout the United States, covering free sites, national and state parks, national forests, and RV parks, and feature numerous details about each location, including prices and amenities, cell phone signal strength, along with reviews from the growing Campendium community.

Some top recommendations from Campendium include Upper Teton View in the Bridger-Teton National Forest; Fort Desoto County Park, just outside Tampa, Florida; Washington Gulch Road, Gunnison National Forest, Colorado; and Forest Road 611, East Rim, Kaibab National Forest, alongside the Grand Canyon.

VIEW ONLINE

CAMPENDIUM.COM

EUROPEAN JOURNEYS

Cool Camping originated from a book released in 2006 by travel writer Jonathan Knight, covering the very best campsites of the English countryside. The resounding success led to a series of books covering the wider Great Britain and extending into other European nations. In 2013, Cool Camping became a fully searchable database with the ability to book your site right then and there. Today Cool Camping lists both campsites as well as glamping options, featuring descriptions and amenities, feedback from those who have stayed there, and information from the campsites themselves. Cool Camping also has a news feed featuring competitions, specials, destination reviews, and essential guides.

Some of Cool Camping's recommendations for camping with your Airstream in Europe include Camping Pré Fixe in the Midi-Pyrenees of France; Domaine de Pradines, Lanuéjols, in the beautiful French countryside; Lanefoot Farm in the Lake District, England; and Camping Alpe di Siusi, in the stunning Dolomites mountain range of northern Italy.

VIEW ONLINE

COOLCAMPING.CO.UK

Dolomites mountain range of northern Italy, a must see on your Airstream travels in Europe.

AUSTRALIA AND NEW ZEALAND JOURNEYS

Australia and New Zealand are also top spots to take your Airstream on a journey. Locals in both countries consider camping as part of an essential summer activity, so they offer beautiful campsites in some of the most exquisite locations.

In Australia, the WikicampsAustralia app is a user-generated database, featuring details and reviews of campsites, and a chat forum. Wikicamps is also available in New Zealand, the United States, Canada, and the UK.

The New Zealand Motor Caravan Association just turned sixty, and is a great club. It offers discounts from corporate partners, a wonderful community, and brilliant resources. If you are looking for an online interactive version, check out the CamperMate app available on iTunes and for Android. If you're lucky enough to venture that far south, New Zealand's Lake Tekapo and Lake Pukaki are at the top of anyone's best places to camp.

Lake Pukaki, New Zealand, is a very special place to visit with your Airstream.

Mali Mish, a full-time Airstream family of five, enjoys a dust storm while boondocking with their Airstream friends.

LIVING THE AIRSTREAM LIFE

LIVING THE AIRSTREAM LIFE

The Airstream way of life is a unique one; it's one many aspire to, and one that many live every day. The freedom of the open road, the kindred spirits you meet along the way, and the separation from what you are told you should be— these call to the wandering nomad within us all. Airstreams are a catalyst, a starting point for you and your family to feel comfortable and safe on the new journey you are about to embark on.

The following pages feature those who have lived the Airstream way of life for several years. Talking to these people about their experiences and soaking in the knowledge that they can share with all of us can help us turn our own dreams into reality.

BOB WHEELER, PRESIDENT AND CEO OF AIRSTREAM

"THE AIRSTREAM TRAILER GIVES PEOPLE THE COURAGE TO LIVE A LIFE ON THE ROAD. I LOVE THAT ABOUT OUR BRAND. IT IS AN ENABLER FOR TRAVEL AND ADVENTURE. IT ALLOWS PEOPLE JUST ENOUGH COMFORT THAT THEY CAN MAKE THAT LEAP. ONCE THEY DO IT, THEY ALWAYS SAY THE SAME THING: I SHOULD HAVE DONE THIS TEN YEARS AGO."

Above: Mali Mish family, making the most of the Airstream life.
Opposite: Part of the Wand'rly family, son Winter studies up on his storybooks in their vintage Airstream.

"AT THE TIME I JUST THOUGHT MAYBE I COULD DO A LITTLE MAGAZINE ABOUT AIRSTREAMS. IT HADN'T CROSSED MY MIND THAT I WOULD BECOME A CENTRAL FIGURE IN THE AIRSTREAM COMMUNITY. AS A MATTER OF FACT, I WAS THINKING QUITE THE OPPOSITE, I JUST WANTED TO SHARE THE EXPERIENCES OF OTHERS."

RICH LUHR

Some have said Rich Luhr is filling the shoes of Wally Byam as the pied piper of the Airstream community. He publishes *Airstream Life* magazine, organizes Alumapalooza events, and writes books to help Airstream newbies find their feet in Airstreaming. Although, in 2002, he had never even heard of Airstream. Rich had always had a fascination with travel and the outdoors, and spent much of his available time camping with his wife, Eleanor. In 2003, their daughter, Emma, was born, and camping in a tent with a newborn baby wasn't really an ideal option.

They began to look for something child-friendly that still allowed them to travel and enjoy the great outdoors. It was then that Rich discovered vintage Airstreams. They were beautiful, had a great community around them, and at the time were relatively inexpensive. Even though they didn't have a tow vehicle, Rich and Eleanor set out on their search to purchase a vintage Airstream. In August 2003, they came across a 1986 Caravelle and decided that this was to be their new family trailer. They were having such a great time in

the trailer that by October of that year they had spent the last ten weekends in a row in it, traveling up to Canada and down through the southern states. Unfortunately, winter was arriving, and their newly acquired Airstream had to be packed away for the cold snowy months.

Rich was intent on finding a new flexible way of making an income for the family so that they could travel more often in their Airstream. In December 2003, he decided to leave his job to make a move toward this new way of life. A month later a lightbulb went off: maybe he could do a magazine about Airstreams!

VIEW ONLINE

AIRSTREAMLIFE.COM

The magazine was so successful that it turned into a full-time career: Rich had opportunities to collaborate on events and even writes books on Airstreams. Rich recalls, "It was solidified to me when one night I was having dinner with Bob Wheeler, CEO of Airstream, and I said, 'What you really need, Bob, is a new Wally Byam, someone to inspire and do awesome things around the world that would get everyone to buy Airstreams.' He looked very seriously at me, and he said, 'I have one!' I said, 'Oh no no no,' but that is when I realized I was really deep into this Airstream thing and there was no backing out at that point."

"OF ALL MY GOOD FRIENDS AT THIS TIME IN MY LIFE, A GOOD PORTION OF THEM ARE THOSE I HAVE MET THROUGH AIRSTREAMING. THESE ARE THE FRIENDS WE ARE REALLY CLOSE TO BECAUSE THEY ARE OF THE SAME MIND-SET. WE HAVE HAD SOME VERY FORMATIVE EXPERIENCES AND SOME VERY PERSONAL EXPERIENCES TOGETHER. IT HOOKS YOU TOGETHER IN A WAY THAT YOU JUST DON'T GET BY WORKING AT THE SAME OFFICE, OR BEING MEMBERS OF THE SAME CHURCH, OR BEING NEIGHBORS, OR WHATEVER YOUR AFFILIATIONS ARE IN LIFE."

The Airstream Community

There is no question that the community is a huge draw for people buying an Airstream. You would think that people buy an Airstream because they want to travel and experience the freedom of the open road—and that is true, of course—but there is also a strong desire to be part of something more than just themselves. Airstreams offer the opportunity to meet kindred spirits who share their interest and passion for travel and stepping outside the box.

The sharing of this unique experience and lifestyle unquestionably creates a bond. Airstreamers share the world as their living room. When you eat dinner at a picnic table, or hike a mountain together, you share dreams and experiences and really get to know someone. It's part of the cement that holds the Airstream community together.

"The great thing is that when you do meet friends traveling, you don't have to see them every day for the friendship to stay solid," Rich says. "Other friendships can go stale when you move away because the real bonding element was the proximity. With these folks proximity doesn't matter, 'cause they are always moving too!"

MALI MISH

Dan and Marlene have three beautiful children who have been brought up in the full-timer lifestyle, although this wasn't quite their intention from the beginning. The initial idea in purchasing a trailer was to connect as a family and spend time with their children. The outdoor lifestyle really appealed to them, so they bought a teardrop trailer that they planned to take out during the weekends. But this didn't end up suiting their needs, as they wanted to travel for longer than just a weekend and they needed something bigger.

They didn't know much about Airstreams when they bought their 2007 25FB (twenty-five-foot front bedroom) International; it just appealed to them because it had a retro look and "felt well built." Neither did they expect there to be an Airstream community; they thought they would be pretty much alone on their adventures. The plan was to head out on a four-month trip to get their wanderlust out of their system, but as the end of the four months drew near, they felt like they hadn't seen anything. Marlene recalls, "We didn't even touch the surface! We can't stop; we want to keep doing this.

We had to find a way to make it work." The more they traveled the more they wanted to keep traveling. With Dan working as a web developer, it was possible to keep the income coming in as long as they had connection to the Internet. So they made the decision to just "make it work."

VIEW ONLINE

MALIMISH.COM

Social Media

As social media became mainstream (especially with the growing popularity of Instagram), Dan and Marlene had an entirely new way to meet people. They could follow like-minded people who posted their locations and travel images, start conversations, and cross paths. "We were on Instagram pretty early, we were really involved in creating hashtags and making them active." Dan and Marlene followed other Airstreamers and travelers, connected with them, and made plans to meet up on the road. They became a part of a traveling neighborhood. Today, social media is integral to many Airstreamers. Whether it's a group on Facebook or a hashtag on Instagram, it gives them a sense of community—even though the neighbors may be a thousand miles away!

Full-timing with Kids

Lots of families seek out Dan and Marlene for advice on life on the road with a family. When they started out in 2008, it was pretty unusual, but particularly over the last few years it has become a lot more common for families to take to the road. Besides their own wanderlust, Dan and Marlene thought it was important to instill a sense of curiosity, adaptability, and confidence in their children. Marlene said, "We wanted them to feel comfortable with change." The world is changing so fast, and adaptability is one of those key skills that you can teach your children, that will prepare them well for the future.

As many families do on the road, Dan and Marlene are road-schooling their children. The wonderful thing about learning on the road is that the outdoors is your classroom, and instead of looking at pictures of the Grand Canyon in a textbook, you can go and stand on its rim; instead of learning about the history of Rosa Parks in a classroom, you can go sit on the very bus seat she sat on. Dan recalls keeping the kids up until 1:00 a.m. to see the dancing lights of aurora borealis. The next day this was a science lesson for their oldest, but their two younger children will also have experienced and learned something that they will be able to put into context later down the road.

Along with academic education, another key factor of traditional schooling is to socially educate children. Creating social opportunities to bond with other children on the road is just about making the most of the time that you do spend with others. Dan and Marlene will often make a detour in their plans so they can connect with other traveling families, and the children also know to make the most of all opportunities to get to know other kids. The Airstream community offers intergenerational social opportunities: children get to spend time with people of all ages and backgrounds, and become socially confident no matter what the environment.

Practically, the Airstream can get really messy really quickly with a family of five, but it's also pretty quick to clean up given it's such a small space. A key to living harmoniously with a family in a trailer is for everyone to have their own dedicated space: a space where they sleep and keep their books and toys. Because everyone has only a small dedicated space, every family member needs to choose carefully what they wish to keep. Dan says, "It's not like we can just head to a store and buy more stuff. If they really want something, they really have to think about how essential it is and what are they going to have to swap out in its place. It makes them really think about and appreciate what things they do have, and be more conscious about taking care of them."

DAN AND MARLENE

"OUR MAIN AIM IS TO BRING UP OPEN-MINDED, ADAPTABLE, ADVENTUROUS KIDS."

"TRAVELING THIS WAY CAN BECOME REALLY ADDICTIVE. SOMETIMES PEOPLE START OUT WITH THE IDEA THAT 'WE WILL TRAVEL FOR A YEAR TO FIND THE PLACE THAT WE WANT TO LIVE,' AND SOMETIMES THAT DOES HAPPEN, BUT I THINK FOR MOST PEOPLE YOU START TO REALIZE THAT THERE IS NOWHERE PERFECT—SO YOU DECIDE INSTEAD TO JUST KEEP SEARCHING."

WAND'RLY

Nathan and Renee met during art school but went their separate ways after graduation. Unbeknownst to them at the time, their wanderlust would bring them back together years later. Nathan began his full-time travels as a solo dad with his son, Tristan. He worked as a freelance Web designer to fund their travels in a "junky RV from the '90s." Renee had followed her own dreams of traveling through Europe, but when Nathan decided to buy a VW bus in her hometown back in America, their paths crossed once again. Renee joined Nathan and Tristan in their newly acquired VW bus, traveling the United States for about a year before Renee became pregnant. Stopping only for a short stint for their son to be born, they jumped back in the van with their new baby on board. Soon son number three was on the way, and they decided they needed a bigger traveling space for their growing family.

They had been admiring Airstreams for a while. Nathan said they "looked cool; they were iconic, sturdy, and real; and appealed much more than a white box. We had always liked older vintage stuff, and settled on purchasing a 1976 thirty-one-foot Excella for our new traveling home." Keen to get traveling again after being in one place for over a year while their third son was born, they did some minor cosmetic renovations and headed back on the road. The Airstream was in okay condition, but over the coming three years they had to do quite a bit of work to it, cosmetic and structural. Doing this work while traveling came with its own challenges, but the family of five was happy to be back out on the open road.

VIEW ONLINE

WANDRLYMAGAZINE.COM

Working on the Road

Funding your travels on the road can be tricky. Freelance work is a great option, but you have to be the type of person who is disciplined enough to do it. It can be difficult when you're sitting on the edge of a beautiful beach or in the middle of a national park to stop and pull out your computer because it's a workday. It's not for everyone, and a lot of people like to have routine: a set time and place where they work, and someone to hold them responsible so they'll do what they need to do.

Some Airstreamers take a completely different tack to make money by saving up and traveling for a year, or selling their house to buy a couple of rentals for the income they need to not have to work on the road at all.

Advice for Embarking on a Full-time Adventure

Given Nathan has an online magazine and is open to talking about living on the road, he usually gets inundated with questions about how to take the next step into this full-time lifestyle. Below are some of his most popular tips for those committed to taking that next step.

Most people say they will go in a year or six months, but then wait until the last minute to buy their trailer and tow vehicle. But Nathan advises, "Ideally you want to be purchasing it as early as possible. You don't want to be figuring how your trailer works (or doesn't work) on the road. You will have enough new challenges, so feeling comfortable with your rig will make those challenges a lot easier to bear." Buy it early, camp in the driveway, take it out for weekends, and get confident and comfortable with your trailer.

Join Instagram. It's the platform that most people who are full-timing use to connect and share, and will help you meet up with other like-minded people.

Meet up with people who have been full-timing for a while, and talk to them about what your concerns are, asking for advice and sharing experiences. People are usually pretty happy to talk and, if they can, help in some way.

It's not a bad idea to learn everything you can about engines, plumbing, electrical systems—so when things don't go according to plan on the road you don't have to break the bank getting things fixed: you have the knowledge to do it yourself.

SHARON PIENIAK

Sharon had been living in the same town for eleven years, and she was restless. In 2007, she took a six-week camping trip driving through the Canadian Maritimes and tenting by herself at night. She came back from that trip inspired: "I loved it so much, I just wanted to live this way all the time." Her friends and family weren't so sure and tried to convince her otherwise.

The appeal of living this way was the ability to move and not become restless. But living in a tent full-time was not very practical. A friend suggested an RV instead. "But I didn't really like RVs," Sharon says. "They were ugly, and the people who had them spent all their time watching TV inside with the air-conditioning on." But then she came across Airstreams, "Airstreams are beautiful and were the perfect solution." Wasting no time, the next day Sharon headed to the Airstream dealer and "just got one!"

Since 2007, Sharon has traveled in her Airstream trailer solo, and has never looked back. "It has been tremendous—I like change; I like new places. People often ask me, 'What are you running away from?' But after years on the road, I have figured out that I was actually running to myself. Being in new places and meeting new people has made me much more confident and feel much more solid in the world."

VIEW ONLINE

JOYRIDESOFAMERICA.COM

As a Solo Traveler

When thinking about traveling solo, there are a couple of things that tend to pop to the front of your mind. Firstly, "Am I going to get lonely on the road?" and secondly, "Am I going to be safe?"

If you are going to travel by yourself, you are probably someone who is already comfortable being alone. Although you may enjoy the company of others, you probably enjoy spending time by yourself too. With social media and the community around Airstream and travelers of any kind, you will have plenty of opportunities to connect if you want to. Sharon found that traveling alone made her more approachable. People tend to talk to those traveling on their own more than they do to couples and families. Sharon also found that being a photographer made it easier to approach people because she had more of a reason for being there, and a starting point for a conversation.

Safety

There were only a handful of times when Sharon felt unsafe, and one of those times she unfortunately managed to damage her trailer: "I had gone down a dead-end road in the middle of Texas. It was dusk, so before too long it was dark. I wanted to turn around and go back, but there was no room to turn around. I tried anyway, and I damaged my trailer in the process. But that was because the prospect of spending the night there did not feel safe, my phone didn't work, and I had to get out of there no matter what. In retrospect I feel I would have been fine, but at the time it was a different story." On a few occasions, when Sharon arrived at a place where she was going to camp for the night, she "just got creeped out" and didn't want to be there. But that's the nice thing about being on wheels: you can just keep driving on to the next spot. "You really learn to trust your gut and trust your instincts," she says.

For a solo traveler (and especially if you're a woman) these situations can be frightening. Sharon has learned to plan ahead and give herself ample time to park, set up, have dinner, and relax in a new spot. She recalls, "I had the rule to always arrive before 2:00 p.m. and to never push it." And definitely don't arrive anywhere in the dark.

But Sharon also found that she was never really alone—there were often people willing to help others, especially a solo traveler. People have a natural inclination to want to help people who are by themselves, and to support them in a time where a little help can go a long way.

Curtis, Aluminarium's furry companion, enjoying a refreshing shower on a hot day. Check out Curtis's adventures on Instagram @aluminarium.

Osa, Kristiana Spaulding's fur baby, loves her travels with her Airstream aficionado mama. Check out her adventures on Instagram @silvertrailer.

A Furry Companion

Many solo travelers have mentioned that traveling with a dog is a huge help. Not only are they wonderful companions, but they also can be a safety feature. Their loud bark is a warning sign to you, and if you have a big dog, it's a warning to others! To Sharon, having a dog makes all the difference to her daily life as a solo traveler.

There are some downsides to traveling with a pet, though. For one thing, it can be restrictive. Dogs can't be in hot climates, so having one will end up dictating your travel plans. Some RV parks or destinations don't allow dogs, and you may also be restricted in the activities you can partake in. When Sharon was staying at the Grand Canyon, she wanted to walk down to the bottom of the canyon, but there was no way she could leave her dog in the hot trailer.

Leaving your dog alone in your trailer is something you should never do for long. You also need to consider the ability to keep it cool. Never rely on your A/C to keep the trailer cool while you're away; they do have a tendency to fail, and that could be fatal to your dog.

Harley, Sharon's furry companion. Check out his adventures on Instagram @joyridesofamerica.

SHARE THE PASSION

BEING PART OF THE AIRSTREAM COMMUNITY

Airstreams have an undeniable following. They continue to gain popularity year after year, and it's no surprise that a strong community has built up around the passion for these trailers and the lifestyle they offer. As soon as you start talking to those who have as much love and passion for Airstreams as you do, you begin to realize that they are not only kindred spirits but also a support network that will want to help you fulfill your own Airstream dream.

Almost one hundred years ago, groups and clubs began forming around travel trailers and the camping lifestyle. Today social media and blogs offer opportunities for like-minded souls to connect, share their knowledge, and meet up along the road. Whether you last saw an Airstreamer two months ago or two years ago, the bond that you have will make you feel like it was just last week. When you are a new member of the Airstreaming community, you are sincerely welcomed with open arms and usually a drink or two at happy hour!

WBCCI International Rally, Farmington, New Mexico, United States, 2015.

SOCIAL MEDIA AND WEBSITES

Instagram

Given Airstreamers are travelers, they yearn to capture and share where they have been and what they have seen. Instagram is a great way to connect with other like-minded travelers, be inspired to visit new places, and form friendships. Many kindred spirits who post on Instagram find a way to connect on the road, cross paths, and meet face-to-face. You don't have to be an organized group or club, just people who share the same wanderlust.

Air Forums

If you are looking for technical information, an upcoming rally, or the history on your trailers, Air Forums can help you out. Just pop a key word in the search bar and you are pretty much guaranteed to find an answer, either from the site hosts or highly experienced Airstream aficionados on the site who are always willing to lend a hand.

AIRFORUMS.COM

Facebook

There are many great groups on Facebook. No matter where you live, you are more than likely to find a group of Airstreamers nearby. One group in particular that is growing with rapid force is Airstream Addicts. Joining Airstream Addicts is like having a twenty-four-hour Airstream hotline: no matter what "stupid" question you ask or what help someone is asking for, they will always respond. Even if you are just proud of the work that you have done on your trailer and you want to share it with someone who understands what it means to you, post it there! Formed in 2015, Airstream Addicts now has thousands of members from all over the world. It is an easy-access, nonjudgmental group for those who love the Airstream, whether you have one or just dream of having one!

RALLIES AND EVENTS

Alumapalooza

Every year the Alumapalooza event is held at the Airstream factory in Jackson Center, Ohio. This is an extra-special rally because not only does it offer you the opportunity to meet some of your fellow Airstreamers but also it's based at the factory, and you get the chance to get a great understanding of Airstream history and how the trailers are made. Alumapalooza runs from the end of May through the beginning of June, and offers hands-on workshops, talks, opportunities to provide feedback to Airstream, and the all-important "rivet race": How fast can you rivet those aluminum panels? Hosted by Rich Luhr and Brett Greiveldinger (editor and marketing director, respectively, of *Airstream Life* magazine), this event is one to put on your calendar!

ALUMAPALOOZA.COM

WBCCI

Every year in July, the Wally Byam Caravan Club International (WBCCI) holds an international rally. It brings all the WBCCI units together, including the Vintage Airstream Club. Both clubs offer many events and rallies throughout the year. Check out your local chapter's website to get the details on the next one coming up. There are also many international WBCCI groups forming, including WBCCI Europe. They offer fantastic caravans too, just like Wally and Helen used to organize, so go join your fellow travelers on the road in a stream of Airstreams!

WBCCI.ORG

VINTAGEAIRSTREAMCLUB.COM

Tin Can Tourists

Tin Can Tourists was formed back in 1919, when camping and travel trailers were beginning to make a big impact on the holiday choices. Tin Can Tourists today consists of a variety of vintages trailers and motor homes, offering fantastic rallies and events. Tin Can Tourists is a great way to grow your community outside the Airstream family, and share in the love of all trailers and motor homes of yesteryear.

TINCANTOURISTS.COM

Other Fantastic Events

Balloon Fiesta National Rally, Albuquerque, New Mexico.

Modernism Week, Palm Springs, California.

Pismo Vintage Trailer Rally, Pismo Beach, California.

MAGAZINES, BOOKS, AND DOCUMENTARIES

Airstream Life

An essential for any Airstreamer is *Airstream Life* magazine. It is released quarterly and is full of stories and insights about the Airstream life, along with practical tips and advice. You can subscribe to the paper copy or download to your iPad.

AIRSTREAMLIFE.COM

Alumination

If you would like to know more about the Airstream community, Eric Bricker has spent three years interviewing and documenting the community of Airstreamers. His documentary *Alumination* is an essential must-see for any Airstream fan.

ALUMINATIONMOVIE.COM

Wand'rly

Wand'rly is an online magazine written by full-time traveler Nathan Swartz about his experiences with his partner, Renee, and their three children, sometimes joined by Renee's mom, making a family of six, and offering advice on full-time travel. Nathan offers great insight as well as realistic practicalities of living on the road.

WANDRLYMAGAZINE.COM

Essential Books

You can also purchase an array of books about Airstreams, from the history of Airstream to how to renovate an Airstream. The two most highly recommended for the newbie Airstreamer are *The Newbies Guide to Airstreaming* and *Airstream Life's (Nearly) Complete Guide to Airstream Maintenance*, both by Rich Luhr, full-time traveler for many years and editor and publisher of *Airstream Life* magazine. Rich lives the Airstream life hook, line, and sinker, and is a great guide to the adventure you are embarking on.

NOT QUITE READY TO COMMIT?

STILL DECIDING?

Whether you are still deciding what type of Airstream you would like, or you love the idea and want to try it out but can't see it as a permanent part of your lifestyle, you can find many ways to be part of the Airstream way of life. As Airstreams become more popular, and the Airstream bed-and-breakfast option becomes more mainstream, it's very easy to rent an Airstream set up with all the bells and whistles you could hope for in a stunning location.

Staying in an Airstream really gives you a feel for how the interior space works, but for the more adventurous types who want to see what it's really like to tow your home behind you and set it up in your choice of location, there is another option. There is a company that provides you with not only an Airstream fitted out with luxurious linens and high-spec features, but also a tow vehicle, lessons on how to tow an Airstream, and a customized itinerary.

AIRSTREAM 2 GO

Dicky Riegel was president and CEO of Airstream and also worked for Thor Industries, Airstream's parent company, for many years. While he was CEO, he was often asked, "Wow, Airstreams are cool—how do I rent one?" This question stuck with Dicky and was the inspiration for his new Airstream-inspired business, Airstream 2 Go. The idea was founded on making Airstreams more accessible to those who have fallen in love with the silver bullet but for one reason or another can't own one.

The two main constraints for many would-be owners are time and space. If you have a regular nine-to-five job, your vacation days are probably limited to two weeks a year. When it comes to investing in an Airstream and an accompanying tow vehicle, many can't justify the investment given the limited time they have available for it. The other constraint is storage space. Many city dwellers just don't have the extra-long driveway or the extra garage space to store those vehicles during the year. This makes the experience that Airstream 2 Go offers ideal to many.

Airstream 2 Go's clientele are adventurous in spirit, ranging from families to couples and friends, as well as a few who want to try before they buy. As any newbie Airstreamer will tell you, the first time you tow is always a little nerve-racking, and setting up can sometimes be a little daunting, but Airstream 2 Go has many clients who have never driven a trailer before. The company offers in-depth instruction and instills you with confidence before you head out on the road. They also offer to plan a trip for you, down to every little detail, so all you need to do is enjoy living the Airstream life.

VIEW ONLINE

AIRSTREAM2GO.COM

UNITED STATES ACCOMMODATION

Airstreams in Malibu

Murray and Kay have a stunning twenty-acre property atop the Malibu hills, with 360-degree views from the Pacific Ocean to the Santa Monica Mountains, and there sits a beautifully restored 1957 twenty-two-foot Flying Cloud. Introducing you to the Airstream way of life, this beautiful trailer, featuring a stunning interior accentuated by the homely furnishings, really gives you a wonderful idea of what it is like to live in an original '50s Airstream. This stunning property is also the home to a 1971 Sovereign Airstream set in a private meadow, underneath the dappled shade of two large trees. Both trailers are in private settings, giving you a wonderful opportunity to feel what it's like to boondock, having nothing but nature for miles.

AIRSTREAM VINTAGE TRAILER ADVENTURE ON AIRBNB.COM

Palm Springs Argosy

The best place to check out what the Painted Airstream is really like is in Palm Springs, California. A beautiful 1972 Argosy, (that is also featured in the DIY chapter), is nestled in the base of the San Jacinto Mountains. The beautifully restored interior by veteran DIYer Kristiana Spaulding, shows you how an original 1970s Airstream interior would have looked back in the day. Positioned in a lovely spot with access to a beautiful pool, cozy Jacuzzi, shuffleboard, and mini gym, *Acacia* the Argosy is a wonderful place to spend the night.

SILVERTRAILER.COM

The Vintages

In the heart of Oregon's wine country sits a very special campground. The Vintages features an array of retro-style trailers, including both modern and vintage Airstreams. Two of the featured Airstream trailers, a 1957 thirty-foot Sovereign of the Road with a modern interior and a 1959 eighteen-foot Globester with an original-style interior, were beautifully renovated by the accomplished designers of Flyte Camp (featured in the professional designers chapter on pages 72–75). The Vintages also features a 2014 twenty-two-foot Bambi Sport; a modern factory interior with retro-styled accessories brings a personal touch to this beautiful Airstream. If you are trying to decide between new or vintage, this is the perfect place to stay, offering you the best of both worlds. Book a night or two in each trailer while you sample the wares of the local vineyards.

THE-VINTAGES.COM

Auto Camp

Auto Camp sits in a prime spot in Santa Barbara, featuring five Airstreams all created by Hofmann Architecture (featured earlier in the professional designers chapter, on pages 68–69). It's a great way to test out the size and era you like as well as experience the craftsmanship of Hofmann Airstreams.

Auto Camp has opened another venue, ninety minutes north of San Francisco, with twenty-four Airstreams set among the redwoods along the Russian River in Guerneville, California.

AUTOCAMP.COM

EUROPE ACCOMMODATION

UK

Vintage Vacations

Starting out as a labor of love and a weekend hobby, Vintage Vacations brought a 1965 Trade Wind over from America to the UK in 2004. Vintage Vacations has now been in business since 2007, offering accommodation in nine different vintage Airstream trailers on a peaceful corner of a working farm, located on the unique Isle of Wight at the southern tip of England. Vintage Vacations features Safaris, Trade Winds, and Overlanders from the 1950s and '60s, with absolutely beautiful and sincerely loved interiors.

VINTAGEVACATIONS.CO.UK

Happy Days Retro Vacations

Happy Days Retro Vacations is a gorgeous vintage Airstream retreat based in Saxmundham, Suffolk. This collection of American Vintage Airstreams has been touched up by British country interior design and creates the sweetest combination while keeping the interiors original as possible. These are a beautiful collection of vintage Airstreams from Dee Dee the 1959 Trade Wind, to the youngest trailer Peggy, a 1973 Trade Wind. A visit here will get you inspired to live your own vintage Airstream dream.

HAPPYDAYSRV.CO.UK

FRANCE

Belrepayre

In the foothills of the Pyrenees in France, Perry and Coline have created a very unique Airstream trailer park. Twelve trailers from the '40s, '50s, '60s, and '70s are nestled within a beautifully landscaped Airstream village. It's a perfect opportunity to experience Airstreams in Europe. It offers not only accommodation, but also RV sites with full hookups. Belrepayre attracts Airstreamers from all over Europe, and has hosted a number of Airstream events, including the WBCCI European Rally of 2016. It gives you many opportunities to meet Airstreamers and immerse yourself in the Airstream community.

AIRSTREAMEUROPE.COM

ITALY

Camping Ca' Savio

When you think of Venice, Italy, you don't necessarily think trailers and campgrounds, but just east of the famous city lies Italy's first Airstream park. With stunning beaches and fabulous food, the Cavallino Peninsula is home to Camping Ca' Savio. With accommodation options from bungalows to tent sites, Camping Ca' Savio has been a family-run business for several generations. In 2015, stepping it up a notch, they decided to import six brand-new 684 International Airstreams to sit pride of place along the beach.

CASAVIO.COM

AUSTRALIA ACCOMMODATION

Happy Glamper's Peggy Sue

Happy Glamper on the Mornington Peninsula in Australia has an extra-special feature. Peggy Sue is a 1966 Trade Wind, with a renovated interior. She is all kitted out and ready to hit the road. Happy Glamper offers to drive Peggy Sue to your favorite location, set her up, and allow you to just enjoy the experience. Not only do they have some wonderful location suggestions, but there is also the option of taking her to your own backyard if you fancy testing out an Airstream in the comforts of your own driveway, or if you are in need of a guesthouse for the weekend. It's a great way to bring the Airstream way of life into your community.

HAPPYGLAMPER.COM.AU

Notel Melbourne

Notel Melbourne is a spectacular urban hotel like you have never seen before. Six renovated Airstreams sit atop a parking building in the middle of Melbourne's CBD. The bright colors, and completely unique bespoke Airstream interiors, are something I can guarantee you won't haven't seen before. If you are looking for an extra-special place to stay in Melbourne, and inspiration for your modern vintage Airstream renovation, make sure Notel is on your to-do list!

NOTELMELBOURNE.COM.AU

SOUTH AFRICA ACCOMMODATION

Grand Daddy

The Grand Daddy is a rooftop Airstream park in central Cape Town, hosting seven vintage Airstreams. Each one's interior is uniquely decorated and inspired by the quintessential South African road trip. If you are looking for some outside-the-box interior design ideas, this would be the place.

GRANDDADDY.CO.ZA

Old Mac Daddy

Old Mac Daddy, a beautiful Airstream park, is set in the exquisite countryside just outside Cape Town, nestled into the hillside. With names like Give Bees a Chance, Mills & Boon, and The Secret Life of Plants, you know the interior design is something quite special. This little secluded paradise is a great place to go for Airstream inspiration.

OLDMACDADDY.CO.ZA

NOW IS THE TIME TO EMBARK ON YOUR OWN AIRSTREAM ADVENTURE

YOUR FIRST STEP

There are many of you out there who are adventurers at heart, but as time passed by, life got in the way. Responsibilities took over, and social expectations defined your path. But that little light of adventure still burns, the one that some days, as you drive to the outskirts of town, makes you just want to keep on driving and find out what's over that hill and around that corner, and leave the routine of the well-worn path of your everyday mantra behind. But even the smallest step to that new path seems too far outside your comfort zone.

Want to know a little secret? That first step is always the hardest, so don't put so much expectation on it. Small steps will still take you toward where you want to go. We tend to have this perception that we need to be all in—or not at all. Not only that but we need to do it now, and we have a need for instant gratification. We live this fast-paced lifestyle, always in a rush to get somewhere, even if we aren't always sure where that is. You can make the decision today that you want to live a life of adventure, and make a long-term plan to make it happen.

Be realistic about what you can take on in these first steps: for some that might be a night in an Airstream hotel, for others that might be deciding on organizing a garage sale of all of your belongings this weekend. Whatever path suits you, just know by reading this book you have now become one of the members of a wonderful community of kindred spirits and lifetime adventurers. Airstreamers are truly one of a kind; they have a never-ending list of where they came from, but a genuine connection in where they are headed.

WITH THANKS

There are many more stories about the Airstream community—these pages only touch the surface but I hope give you an introduction to this special community who live life outside the run of the mill. I would love to thank everyone I met along my travels of making this book; it's been a very special two years that have changed my life, my spirit, and my soul. I found a family in the Airstream community, a place of belonging and comfort, where I met kindred spirits and heard inspiring stories.

If I started to list everyone who has been a part of this wonderful journey I would require an entire book, but I did want to mention one person in particular who didn't explicitly feature in this book but was key to making it happen. Dale Schwamborn is the unofficial historian for Airstream, a family relation to Wally Byam, he grew up as a fundamental part of the Airstream community. He made my journey into the Airstream community a very special one: not only did he share his own story, but he also introduced me to many others who are integral to the Airstream community. He generously gave his time and energy to helping me on this wondrous journey.

Of course key to this story is the Airstream company itself, who have been so supportive in helping me with stories, contacts, and material to tell the story of the Airstream community. In particular, a very special thanks to Peter Orthwein, Bob Wheeler, and Mollie Hansen, who have been integral to the journey of creating this book, believing in its vision and investing their personal time and energy to give me such a special and once-in-a-lifetime experience with Airstream.

The Harper Design team are a strong force of inspirational people who I have had such a pleasure to meet. They believed in me, my vision, and my ability, and have been a fantastic support network through this process. A very special thanks to publisher Marta Schooler, design manager Lynne Yeamans, and last but definitely not least my editor, Rebecca Hunt.

A very special lady I would like to give my sincerest thanks to is Annette Ellis, a very dear friend for many years and also essential to the graphic design of this book. With her energy and design sense this book and its stories have come to life on these pages.

A personal thanks to those who have supported me on this incredible journey, during the lightbulb moments and the writer's block: my incredible family. My mum, Jesse June, who has been there for me through thick and thin and is the most inspirational woman I have ever known—always following her heart, listening to her soul, and grounding her spirit in what she believed was right. She's a very hard act to follow, but I'm very blessed to have such a high bar set to try and reach. My dad, Bruce, who has loved me since the day I was born and has always wanted the best for me. My dad is a traveler, an adventurer, a man who sets his goals and moves toward them with conviction. He is my grounding force to make my own dreams a reality. My brother, Michael, what can I say, he is my best friend, my support network, my inspiration, and my reality check. He is a guiding light in my life, his passion and drive, and his success and sincerity, influence my every day. He has been through all my ups and downs and still he comes out smiling. These three people are the founding in which I am able to find the connection, courage, and strength to achieve anything I set my mind to. Including this book, in which I have put my heart and soul. I hope you enjoy the journey of reading it as much as I enjoyed the journey of writing it.

Much love, Karen xx

Book Credits

Author:	Karen Flett
Publisher:	Marta Schooler
Senior Design Manager:	Lynne Yeamans
Senior Editor:	Rebecca Hunt
Graphic Designer:	Annette Ellis
Airstream Company:	Peter Orthwein
	Bob Wheeler
	Mollie Hansen

Photo Credits

Images reproduced by permission of Airstream, Inc. Pages 14, 15, 16, 17, 18, 19, 28, 32, 33, 35, 37, 41, 43, 45, 48, 51, 54, 55, 56, 110, and 112.

Airstream Odyssey, Page 45.

Alison Turner, Page 128.

Anna M. Scribner, Page 72.

American Retro Caravans, Pages 40, 49, 58, 63, 64, 65, 111, and Back Cover.

Auto Camp, Alex Drysdale, Page 151.

Belrepayre Airstream Trailer Park, Page 153.

Camping Ca' Savio, Page 153.

Caravan Outpost, Page 150.

Christopher Deam, Page 53.

Cool Camping, Page 122.

Dale "Pee Wee" Schwamborn, Page 17.

David Winick, Pages 34, 54, 55, 60, 66, and 67.

Grand Daddy, Page 155.

Happy Days Retro Caravans, by Pete Kyle at UK Aircam, Page 152.

Happy Glamper, Page 154.

The Estate of Helen Byam Schwamborn, Pages 16, 17, 19, and 33.

Hofmann Architecture, Pages 68 and 69.

Junk Gypsy, Amie Sikes, Pages 76, 77, 78, and 79.

Kristiana Spaulding, Pages 85, 88, 89, 91, 97, and 138.

Leigh Wetzel, Pages 117, 119, 121, and 138.

Mali Mish, Dan and Marlene Lin, Pages 124, 126, 130, 131, 133, and Cover.

Vintage Airstream Adventure - Malibu, Pages 46 and 150.

Notel Melbourne, Page 154.

Old Mac Daddy, Page 155.

Peter Orthwein, Page 25.

Rich Luhr, Page 129.

Rowan and Mark Sommerset, Pages 8, 9, and 106.

Sharon Pieniak, Pages 136, 137, and 139.

The Local Branch, Pages 95, 98, 99, and 115.

The Vintages, Pages 57, 73, 74, 75, and 151.

Timeless Travel Trailers / The Fixible Co, Pages 70 and 71.

Vintage Vacations Ltd, Page 152.

Wand'rly **magazine, Nathan Swartz,** Pages 127, 134, and 135.

All other photographs taken by the author, **Karen Flett.**

LIVING THE AIRSTREAM LIFE.

Copyright© 2017 by Karen Flett

Published in 2017 by
Harper Design
An Imprint of HarperCollins*Publishers*
195 Broadway
New York, NY 10007
Tel: (212) 207-7000
Fax: (855) 746-6023
harperdesign@harpercollins.com
www.hc.com

Distributed throughout the world by
HarperCollins*Publishers*
195 Broadway
New York, NY 10007

ISBN 978-0-06-244082-2

Library of Congress Control Number: 2016941260

Front cover photograph: Mali Mish. Dan and Marlene Lin
Back cover photograph: American Retro Caravans Ltd
All other photo credits to the left.

Printed in China

First Printing, 2017